BOSNIA

FRACTURED REGION

BOSNIA

FRACTURED REGION

by Eric Black

Lerner Publications Company / Minneapolis

Website address: www.lernerbooks.com

All maps by Philip Schwartzberg, Meridian Mapping, Minneapolis.
Cover photo © Andree Kaiser/G.A.F.F. Photo Archive
Table of contents photos (from top to bottom) © Kodia Photo &
Graphics; © Federal Committee for Information, Belgrade; © Andree
Kaiser/G.A.F.F. Photo Archive; © Russell Gordon/Zuma Press Inc.;
NATO Photos

Series Consultant: Andrew Bell–Fialkoff
Editorial Director: Mary M. Rodgers
Editor: Chris Dall
Designer: Michael Tacheny
Photo Researcher: Daniel Mesnik

LIBRARY OF CONGRESS CATALOGING-IN-PUBLICATION DATA

Black, Eric
   Bosnia : fractured region / by Eric Black.
   p. cm. — (World in conflict)
   Includes bibliographical references and index.
   Summary: Describes the history of the ethnic conflict in Bosnia,
including current issues.
   ISBN 0-8225-3553-X (lib. bdg. : alk. paper)
1. Yugoslav War, 1991- —Bosnia and Herzegovina—Juvenile
   literature. 2. Bosnia and Herzegovina—History—Juvenile literature.
[1. Yugoslav War 1991- —Bosnia and Herzegovina. 2. Bosnia and
Herzegovina—History.] I. Title. II. Series.
   DR1313.3B58 1999
949.702'4—dc20   96-24951

Manufacture in the United States of America
1 2 3 4 5 6 – JR – 04 03 02 01 00 99

CONTENTS

ABOUT THIS SERIES

Government firepower kills 25 protesters . . . . Thousands of refugees flee the country . . . . Rebels attack capital . . . . Racism and rage flare . . . . Fighting breaks out . . . . Peace talks stall . . . . Bombing toll rises to 52 . . . . Slaughter has cost up to 50,000 lives.

Conflicts between people occur across the globe, and we hear about some of the more spectacular and horrific episodes in the news. But since most fighting doesn't directly affect us, we often choose to ignore it. And even if we do take the time to learn about these conflicts—from newspapers, magazines, television news, or radio—we're often left with just a snapshot of the conflict instead of the whole reel of film.

Most news accounts don't tell you the whole story about a conflict, focusing instead on the attention-grabbing events that make the headlines. In addition, news sources may have a preconceived idea about who is right and who is wrong in a conflict. The stories that result often portray one side as the "bad guys" and the other as the "good guys."

The *World in Conflict* series approaches each conflict with the idea that wars and political disputes aren't simply about bullies and victims. Conflicts are complex problems that can often be traced back hundreds of years. The people fighting one another have complicated reasons for doing so. Fighting erupts between groups divided by ethnicity, religion, and nationalism. These groups fight over power, money, territory, control. Sometimes people who just want to go about their own business get caught up in a conflict just because they're there.

These books examine major conflicts around the world, some of which are very bloody and others that haven't involved a lot of violence. They portray the people involved in and affected by conflicts. They describe how each conflict got started, how it developed, and where it stands. The books also outline some of the ways people have tried to end the conflicts. By reading the stories behind the headlines, you will learn some reasons why people hate and fight one another and, in addition, why some people struggle so hard to end conflicts.

WORDS YOU NEED TO KNOW

autonomous region: An area or territory that is part of a larger political unit but has self-governing powers.

Communist: A person who supports Communism—an economic system in which the government owns the means of producing goods in factories and of growing food.

embargo: A decree prohibiting trade and transportation links to a particular place. An embargo is intended to warn or punish a particular group or to force by economic means an adversary to comply with a government's wishes.

ethnic cleansing: The practice of removing, by armed force or intimidation, the members of another ethnic group from a territory, in order to make that territory ethnically uniform.

ethnic group: A permanent group of people bonded together by a combination of cultural markers, which may include—but are not limited to—race, nationality, tribe, religion, language, customs, and historical origins.

federation: A form of government in which states or groups unite under a central power. The states or groups surrender individual sovereignty but retain limited control over other aspects of government.

nationalist: A person who feels supreme loyalty towards their nation and places a primary emphasis on the promotion of a national culture and national interests.

paramilitary: Describing a supplementary fighting force that often engages in irregular warfare.

propaganda: Ideas, rumor, or information spread to influence people's opinion. The intent of propaganda may be either to injure or to promote an institution, a cause, or a people.

secede: To formally withdraw membership from a political unit, such as a nation, or from an organization, such as the United Nations. The group seeking secession usually desires increased independence or autonomy.

PRONUNCIATION GUIDE

Bosnia-Herzegovina	BAHS-nee-ah Her-tseh-GOH-vih-nah
Croatia	Crow-AY-shah
Croat	CROW-aht
Alija Izetbegovic	AH-lee-yah Ih-zet-BEH-goh-vitch
Radovan Karadzic	RAH-doh-van KAH-rah-jitch
Slobodan Milosevic	Sloh-BOH-dahn Mee-LOH-sheh-vitch
Franjo Tudjman	FRAHN-yoh TOOJ-man

FOREWORD

by Andrew Bell-Fialkoff

Conflicts between various groups are as old as time. Peoples and tribes around the world have fought one another for thousands of years. In fact our history is in great part a succession of wars—between the Greeks and the Persians, the English and the French, the Russians and the Poles, and many others. Not only do states or ethnic groups fight one another, so do followers of different religions—Catholics and Protestants in Northern Ireland, Christians and Muslims in Bosnia, and Buddhists and Hindus in Sri Lanka. Often ethnicity, language, and religion—some of the main distinguishing elements of culture—reinforce one another in characterizing a particular group. For instance, the vast majority of Greeks are Orthodox Christian and speak Greek; most Italians are Roman Catholic and speak Italian. Elsewhere, one cultural aspect predominates. Serbs and Croats speak dialects of the same language but remain separate from one another because most Croats are Catholics and most Serbs are Orthodox Christians. To those two groups, religion is more important than language in defining culture.

We have witnessed an increasing number of conflicts in modern times—why? Three reasons stand out. One is that large empires—such as Austria-Hungary, Ottoman Turkey, several colonial empires with vast holdings in Asia, Africa, and America, and, most recently, the Soviet Union—have collapsed. A look at world maps from 1900, 1950, and 1998 reveals an ever-increasing number of small and medium-sized states. While empires existed, their rulers suppressed many ethnic and religious conflicts. Empires imposed order, and local resentments were mostly directed at the central authority. Inside the borders of empires, populations were multiethnic and often highly mixed. When the empires fell apart, world leaders found it impossible to establish political frontiers that coincided with ethnic boundaries. Different groups often claimed territories inhabited by others. The nations created on the lands of a toppled empire were saddled with acute border and ethnic problems from their very beginnings.

The second reason for more conflicts in modern times stems from the twin ideals of freedom and equality. In the United States, we usually think of freedom as "individual freedom." If we all have equal rights, we are free. But if you are a member of a minority group and feel that you are being discriminated against, your group's rights and freedoms are also important to you. In fact, if you don't have your "group freedom," you don't have full individual freedom either.

After World War I (1914–1918), the allied western nations, under the guidance of U.S. president Woodrow Wilson, tried to satisfy group rights by promoting minority rights. The spread of frantic nationalism in the 1930s, especially among disaffected ethnic minorities, and the catastrophe of World War II (1939–1945) led to a fundamental reassessment of the Wilsonian philosophy. After 1945 group rights were downplayed on the assumption that guaranteeing individual rights would be sufficient. In later decades, the collapse of multiethnic nations like Czechoslovakia, Yugoslavia, and the Soviet Union—coupled with the spread of nationalism in those regions—came as a shock to world leaders. People want democracy and individual rights, but they want their group rights, too. In practice, this means more conflicts and a cycle of secession, as minority ethnic groups seek their own sovereignty and independence.

The fires of conflict are often further stoked by the media, which lavishes glory and attention on independence movements. To fight for freedom is an honor. For every Palestinian who has killed an Israeli, there are hundreds of Kashmiris, Tamils, and Bosnians eager to shoot at their enemies. Newspapers, television and radio news broadcasts, and other media play a vital part in fomenting that sense of honor. They magnify each crisis, glorify rebellion, and help to feed the fire of conflict.

The third factor behind increasing conflict in the world is the social and geographic mobility that modern society enjoys. We can move anywhere we want and can aspire—or so we believe—to be anything we wish. Every day the television tantalizingly dangles the prizes that life can offer. We all want our share. But increased mobility and ambition also mean increased competition, which leads to antagonism. Antagonism often fastens itself to ethnic, racial, or religious differences. If you are an inner-city African American and your local grocer happens to be Korean American, you may see that individual as different from yourself—an intruder—rather than as a person, a neighbor, or a grocer. This same feeling of "us" versus "them" has been part of many an ethnic conflict around the world.

Many conflicts have been contained—even solved—by wise, responsible leadership. But unfortunately, many politicians use citizens' discontent for their own ends. They incite hatred, manipulate voters, and mobilize people against their neighbors. The worst things happen when neighbor turns against neighbor. In Bosnia, in Rwanda, in Lebanon, and in countless other places, people who had lived and worked together and had even intermarried went on a rampage, killing, raping, and robbing one another with gusto. If the appalling carnage teaches us anything, it is that we should stop seeing one another as hostile competitors and enemies and accept one another as people. Most importantly, we should learn to understand why conflicts happen and how they can be prevented. That is why *World in Conflict* is so important—the books in this series will help you understand the history and inner dynamics of some of the most persistent conflicts of modern times. And understanding is the first step to prevention. ⊕

INTRODUCTION

From 1992 to 1995, Bosnia, a small republic in south central Europe, was engulfed by a war that claimed the lives of more than 250,000 people. The conflict forced more than two million people from their homes. Atrocities—including mass murder and rape—were committed on a scale not seen in Europe since World War II (1939–1945). The war made Bosnia infamous for death and ethnic hatred. But before 1992, most of us had scarcely heard of Bosnia.

Bosnia is a former republic of Yugoslavia, a **federation** of republics that violently broke apart in 1991. Serbia, Montenegro, Macedonia, Croatia, and Slovenia are the other republics that made up the Yugoslav federation. Bosnia is a small, triangle-shaped country that covers 51,129 square miles. It is slightly smaller than the state

of Louisiana. Bosnia's prewar population of 4.5 million was close to the population of Minnesota. Much of Bosnia's terrain is mountainous and covered with forests, but the north is composed of flat, arable farmland.

During peacetime most of the territory and population of Bosnia are devoted to agriculture. Bosnian farmers grow wheat, corn, potatoes, and fruit in the region's fertile soil. The terrain of the north has good pasture for sheep herding. A number of rivers—including the Bosna, the Drina, the Neretva, and the Vrbas—crisscross Bosnia. While most of these rivers are not navigable, they are an important source of hydroelectric power. The country is also rich in natural resources. Large forests in the north produce timber, and miners extract copper, lead, zinc, iron ore, and coal from

vast reserves. These resources support Bosnia's heavy industry.

Although a majority of the population of Bosnia lives in rural areas, several cities exist. The largest is Sarajevo, the Bosnian capital. Other major population centers include Mostar, Banja Luka, and Tuzla. After World War II, the Yugoslav government built important factories in a few medium-sized Bosnian cities. These factories produce electric appliances and textiles. There are also iron and steel plants in the town of Zenica, as well as a few important weapons factories.

Facing page:
Although the worst fighting has occurred in Bosnia, ethnic conflict has touched other regions of the former Yugoslavia, including the Republic of Croatia and the province of Kosovo.

SLOVENIA

HUNGARY

ROMANIA

Drava R.

○ ZAGREB

CROATIA

Sava R.

Vojvodina

Novi Sad ●

• Bihac

D i n a r i c

Banja Luka ◉

BOSNIA-
HERZEGOVINA

● Tuzla

Una R.

Vrbas R.

Srebrenica ●

Drina R.

BELGRADE ○

YUGOSLAVIA

Bosna R.

Zepa ●

SERBIA

Morava R.

Danube R.

SARAJEVO ○ ● Pale

A l p s

Neretva R.

Gorazde ●

Mostar ●

MONTENEGRO

Pristina ●

Kosovo

Titograd ◉

A D R I A T I C   S E A

ALBANIA

MACEDONIA

○ SARAJEVO   Capital
◉ Banja Luka   Major City
● Gorazde   Minor City

SERBIA   Republic name
Vojvodina   Province name

–··–··–   International border

––––––   Republic or
    Province boundary

over 5,000 feet
3,000 feet
1,000 feet
sea level

0   20   40   60   80   100 miles

0 20 40 60 80 100 kilometers

Nestled at the foot of the Dinaric Alps along the winding Neretva River, the town of Mostar in southwestern Bosnia was one of the country's most picturesque cities.

For most of the twentieth century, Bosnia was not a separate country at all. It was one of the six republics that made up Yugoslavia, a nation formed after World War I (1914–1918) as a federation of territories inhabited by several South Slavic **ethnic groups.** The six republics are located on the Balkan Peninsula, a region that also includes Albania, Bulgaria, Greece, and parts of Turkey. The word *balkan* is Turkish for "mountain," and the name refers to the numerous mountain ranges that run through the region.

THE REPUBLICS

Serbia, the biggest and most powerful of the former Yugoslav republics, covers most of Bosnia's eastern border. During Yugoslavia's seven decades of existence, the issue of Serbian dominance—or the fear of Serbian dominance—consumed Yugoslavia's internal politics. Located within Serbia are two **autonomous regions,** Kosovo and Vojvodina, both of which contain substantial populations of non-Serbs. The city of Belgrade, the capital of Serbia, was also the capital of the former Yugoslavia.

Slovenia, located in the northwestern corner of the former Yugoslavia, is the wealthiest of the former republics and in 1991 was the first to successfully leave the Yugoslav federation. Slovenia borders Italy, Austria, and Hungary. Physically and culturally, Slovenia is closer to western Europe than are the other republics.

Just south of Slovenia is Croatia, second in size and power among the former Yugoslav republics. Shaped like a pair of pincers, Croatia loops around northern and western Bosnia. The Adriatic Sea borders Croatia to the west. Croatia won its independence from Yugoslavia in a short but brutal war in 1991.

Montenegro, a smaller territory, borders Bosnia on the southeast and has been Serbia's most reliable ally. While four of the former Yugoslav republics are considered independent states, Serbia and Montenegro remain together in a smaller federation that still calls itself Yugoslavia. Media sources sometimes call this smaller federation "rump Yugoslavia," because it is all that is left of what was once a bigger country.

In the far south of the former Yugoslavia, surrounded by Albania, Greece, Bulgaria, and Serbia, sits Macedonia, a small and poor nation that declared its independence from Yugoslavia in 1991. Many observers fear that if the fighting in the former Yugoslavia spreads any farther than it already has, Macedonia is a likely future victim. Macedonia has no border with Bosnia.

Among these republics sits Bosnia. Its full name before the war—the Republic of Bosnia-Herzegovina—refers to two territories that were distinct long ago but that have been ruled jointly for many centuries. Bosnia, the larger of the two

territories, makes up four-fifths of the total country. Herzegovina makes up roughly the southern one-fifth of the country. Media sources typically refer to the republic as just "Bosnia."

ETHNIC GROUPS

For the most part, a single ethnic group dominates the individual republics of the former Yugoslavia. For example, Slovenia is made up mostly of ethnic Slovenes. Serbia is populated mostly by ethnic Serbs, while ethnic Croats dominate Croatia. Montenegro and Macedonia are slightly more diverse than these republics, yet they are still populated predominantly by ethnic Montenegrins and

A Bosnian shepherd moves his flock along a mountain road. Before the war, many rural Bosnians made their livelihood from agriculture.

ethnic Macedonians. While all of these ethnic groups come from the same Slavic family, they each have their own identity.

Each ethnic group is associated with a particular religion. Serbs, Montenegrins, and Macedonians practice the Orthodox variant of Christianity, while most Croats and Slovenes adhere to the Roman Catholic faith. But Bosnia is also home to a significant population of Muslims, descendants of Slavic peoples who converted to the Islamic religion during the rule of the Ottoman Empire.

In several instances, the ethnic groups also have distinct languages. Ethnic Slovenes not only make up the majority population of Slovenia, but they speak a Slovenian language that is distinct from other Slavic languages. Macedonians communicate with a language that is related to Bulgarian. Serbs and Croats speak the same language—called Serbo-Croatian—but they write it with different alphabets. Serbs traditionally use the Cyrillic alphabet, which is used to write Russian, while Croatians use the Latin alphabet—the basis for English.

Bosnia is the only former republic without a dominant ethnic group, thereby making it unique among the other republics. In the country's last census—in 1991—44 percent of Bosnia's 4.5 million people identified themselves as Muslims, 31 percent as Serbs, and 17 percent as Croats. Bosnia also includes a small number of Jews, Roma (often called Gypsies), and Albanians. Muslims outnumber the other groups, but not by an overwhelming margin. All the Bosnian peoples speak the Serbo-Croatian language.

Neither does Bosnia have a dominant religion. Bosnian Serbs are mostly followers of the Serbian Orthodox Church, Bosnian Croats are mostly Roman Catholic, and Bosnian Muslims follow the Islamic faith. In most contexts, the term *Muslim* is a religious description, not an

This road sign in Montenegro, like those in Serbia, uses the Cyrillic alphabet. Serbs and Croats speak different variations of the Serbo-Croatian language, and they also write it differently. Croats use the Latin alphabet.

© Brian Beck

ethnic one. Most Arabs and Turks, many Asians, and some Africans follow Islam, although they represent different ethnic groups. In Bosnia, however, the term Muslim represents both a religion and an ethnicity, separating that group from the Bosnian Serbs and Bosnian Croats. Many Bosnian Muslims, in fact, do not actively practice the Islamic religion.

Before the war, the different ethnic groups in Bosnia lived together peacefully. Population patterns showed that Bosnia was a truly mixed society. Many had begun to identify themselves not as Bosnian Serbs, Bosnian Croats, or Bosnian Muslims, but simply as Bosnians. The people of Bosnia were descended from the same stock, spoke the same language, and looked no different from one another. In cities like Sarajevo, which hosted the 1984 Winter Olympics, visitors found Christian Orthodox churches next to Catholic churches and Islamic mosques (places of worship). Bosnian Serbs, Bosnian Croats, and Bosnian Muslims were friends, neighbors, and sometimes members of the same family.

© Kodia Photo & Graphics

An Islamic mosque and minaret (tower) rise above the old quarter of Sarajevo, the Bosnian capital. Bosnian Muslims built many of the city's mosques during the rule of the Ottoman Empire. Numerous Orthodox Christian and Roman Catholic churches are also located in Sarajevo.

The government of the Republic of Bosnia-Herzegovina, which tried to represent the ethnic diversity of its people, was headed by a seven-member collective presidency that included Bosnian Croats, Bosnian Serbs, and Bosnian Muslims. The Bosnian government also included a 130-member Chamber of Citizens and a

© Kodia Photo & Graphics

Yugoslav athletes observed the lighting of the torch during the opening ceremonies of the 1984 Winter Olympics, held in Sarajevo.

110-member Chamber of Municipalities. This system ensured that all groups were represented equally.

MODERN YUGOSLAVIA

In its original form, Yugoslavia was a monarchy ruled by a Serbian royal family. Yet after World War II, Yugoslavia became a **Communist** nation. Communism is a sytem in which the government closely controls politics and the economy. Under a constitution passed in 1946, Yugoslavia was organized as a federal state, which meant that the powers of government were shared between the central government and

the republics. Yugoslavia's official name became the Socialist Federal Republic of Yugoslavia.

Between the end of World War II and the early 1990s, Europe was divided into a Communist bloc, led by the Soviet Union, and a non-Communist bloc. Marshal Tito, the wily dictator who ruled Yugoslavia for most of this period, implemented a variation of Communism— one that emphasized the management of factories by their own workers, rather than by the government. Unlike other eastern European Communist countries, Yugoslavia did not follow the

orders of the Soviet Union. Yugoslavia's independent stance enabled it to trade with and receive aid from the United States and western Europe.

During the 1950s and 1960s, Yugoslavia was one of the most successful Communist nations in Europe. Tito juggled the demands of Yugoslavia's various ethnic groups so that ethnic differences were downplayed and no single group had more control than another.

The Yugoslavia that existed under Tito, however, slowly disintegrated after the death of the dictator in 1980. During the 1980s, relations between the various ethnic groups of Yugoslavia grew increasingly hostile as the federation's economic problems mounted. Rapid inflation, massive unemployment, and a decrease in the standard of living put a strain on the Yugoslav federation that could not be relieved by economic reforms.

The event that accelerated the breakup of Yugoslavia was the downfall of Communism. In 1989 Communist parties in East Germany, Czechoslovakia, Poland, and Hungary began to lose power over the governments that they had ruled for more than four decades. In 1991 the Communist party of the Soviet Union relinquished its power. The demise of the Communist party in Yugoslavia soon followed. Thereafter, each of the six republics pursued a separate path.

HOW THE TROUBLE BEGAN

In 1991 the republics of Slovenia and Croatia **seceded** from Yugoslavia, because they no longer wanted to be part of the federation. The secession of these two republics seemed to destroy the formula that had enabled Serbs, Croats, and Muslims to live together peacefully in Bosnia. The logic went something like this. The Serbs, the largest and strongest ethnic group in Yugoslavia, were not quite strong enough to dominate all of Yugoslavia's other ethnic groups. The non-Serbian groups, including the Muslims and Croats of Bosnia, thus felt reasonably safe within the Yugoslav federation. But when Croatia and Slovenia seceded from the federation, the Yugoslavia that remained would have been dominated by Serbs. Therefore, the Muslims and Croats of Bosnia over-whelmingly favored the republic's secession from Yugoslavia as well.

To many Bosnian Serbs, the logic was just the opposite. As long as they were part of a larger country—Yugoslavia—in which Serbs were the strongest group, they didn't mind being a minority within Bosnia. But if Bosnia became independent, Bosnia's Serbs would be subject to Bosnian Muslim domination. The Bosnian Serb community found this prospect intolerable and announced that if Bosnia seceded from Yugoslavia, it would secede from Bosnia. Bosnia's Serbs were encouraged by Serbian **nationalists** who advocated the creation of a state that would encompass all territory inhabited by ethnic Serbs.

The government and army of the Republic of Bosnia-Herzegovina opposed the breakup of Bosnia and therefore opposed the secession of the Bosnian Serbs. Although led by a Muslim president, the government of prewar Bosnia did not represent one of the ethnic groups against the others. Throughout the conflict, the government stood for the preservation of an independent, multiethnic Bosnia.

Like the Bosnian Serbs, some Bosnian Croats also harbored a desire to secede from Bosnia and form a tiny state of their own, which they called Herceg-Bosna. During parts of the conflict, Bosnian Croats fought against the Bosnian government. At other times, Bosnian Croats joined forces with the government against the Bosnian Serbs.

It is important to note that not all of Bosnia's Serbs, Croats, and Muslims have been—or want to be—involved in this conflict. Not all Bosnian Serbs are Serbian nationalists, nor do all Bosnian Croats want to secede from Bosnia. Yet many fear that the conflict that began in 1992 may have destroyed the ability of Bosnia's ethnic groups to live together. ⊕

MAJOR PLAYERS IN THE CONFLICT

EU Emblem

European Union (EU) Formerly known as the European Community—which was established to strengthen economic ties among its members—this organization requires its European member-countries to unite in many realms. The EU took its current name in 1993, when its control expanded to include military matters, law enforcement, and immigration. Countries applying for EU membership must meet strict EU standards in economic and human rights practices.

Izetbegovic, Alija Elected as the head of the rotating presidency of Bosnia-Herzegovina in 1990. During the war, Izetbegovic acted as the president of Bosnia-Herzegovina and the leader of Bosnia's Muslims. In 1996 voters chose him to be the chairperson of Bosnia's three-member presidency.

Karadzic, Radovan The main spokesperson for the Bosnian Serbs, Karadzic became the president of Republika Srpska in 1991 and directed the Bosnian Serb war effort.

Milosevic, Slobodan Served as the president of Serbia from 1989 to 1997. In mid-1997, the Serbian parliament appointed Milosevic as the president of Yugoslavia.

Alija Izetbegovic

Radovan Karadzic

North Atlantic Treaty Organization (NATO) Formed in 1949 by European and North American countries to provide mutual defense against attacks by the Soviet Union or any other aggressor. During the Bosnian war, NATO took part in military operations against the Bosnian Serbs, and in 1995 NATO assumed responsibility for peacekeeping operations in the republic.

Tudjman, Franjo Elected as president of Croatia in 1990, he advocated and guided the republic's secession from Yugoslavia in 1991.

UN Emblem

United Nations (UN) A nongovernmental agency set up in 1945 to work for world peace. In 1991 the UN negotiated a cease-fire in Croatia, and in 1992 the organization began humanitarian operations to aid refugees in Bosnia.

United Nations Protection Force (UNPROFOR) A peacekeeping force created by the UN Security Council in 1991. UNPROFOR troops have served in Croatia and Bosnia.

Slobodan Milosevic

Yugoslav People's Army—Jugoslovenska Narodna Armija (JNA) The armed forces of the Yugoslav federation, established to protect the state from external threats. With an officer corps dominated by ethnic Serbs, the JNA played a major role in both the Croatian and Bosnian wars.

Franjo Tudjman

CHAPTER

1

THE RECENT CONFLICT AND ITS EFFECTS

The Bosnian war began in early 1992, just a few days after the republic had officially seceded from Yugoslavia. To defend the Serbian population of Bosnia against the perceived threat of Muslim domination, Bosnian Serb forces began a military campaign to secure all territory inhabited by Bosnian Serbs. It quickly appeared that they would easily achieve their goal. Within months the Bosnian Serb forces had occupied nearly two-thirds of the republic, easily defeating the poorly armed Bosnian army, a civilian militia made up mostly of Bosnian Muslims and Bosnian Croats. The Bosnian Serbs' ultimate goal was to carve out a Serbian state—called the Republika Srpska—that could eventually join with the Republic of Serbia.

If all of the Bosnian Serbs had lived in a single region of Bosnia and if they had had that region to themselves, the issue of secession might have been solved in a less violent manner. But the population patterns in prewar Bosnia were too complex. Bosnian Serb majorities mixed with large minorities of Bosnian Muslims and Bosnian Croats across the countryside. In addition, small-to medium-sized cities with Bosnian Muslim majorities were surrounded by countryside that was heavily populated by Bosnian Serbs.

ETHNIC CLEANSING

In pursuing their military goals, the Bosnian Serbs felt they could not tolerate non-Serb peoples in Bosnian Serb towns. Bosnian Serb forces used murder, rape, and terror to drive Bosnian Muslims, Bosnian Croats, and people of mixed heritage out of the towns to make these areas ethnically uniform. The Bosnian Serb leadership referred to these practices as **ethnic cleansing.**

Ethnic cleansing took place in many towns and cities throughout Bosnia, but a single case study may show how it worked in practice. Banja Luka, the second-largest of Bosnia's cities, is a commercial and industrial center and the major agricultural market town serving north central Bosnia. This area is the heart of the mainly Serb region of Bosnia called the Bosanska Krajina. Before the war, Banja Luka's population of 143,000 was divided into roughly equal numbers of Bosnian Serbs and Bosnian Muslims, with a smaller number of Bosnian Croats. Soon after the war began, Bosnian Serb **paramilitary** forces—aided by the Serb-dominated Yugoslav People's Army (JNA)—took control of the city. The new author-

A Bosnian Serb soldier peers out from his foxhole in the trenches surrounding the city of Sarajevo. The heavy weaponry of the JNA allowed Bosnian Serb forces to conquer nearly 70 percent of Bosnian territory within the first few months of the war.

ities subjected Banja Luka's Muslims to ever-increasing levels of persecution. First, they removed Bosnian Muslims from top jobs in government and industry, then from any job with decision-making authority. They then turned many Muslims out of their homes. Banja Luka's ethnic Croats re-ceived similar treatment. Bosnian Serb paramilitary forces created an atmosphere of terror and intimidation for anyone who was not a Bosnian Serb.

Following this early phase of ethnic cleansing, many non-Serb men received no-tices drafting them into the Bosnian Serb paramilitary. If they entered the military, they would have to fight against their own ethnic kin. If they resisted the draft, those who still had jobs or homes would lose them for draft resistance. The third option was to flee, a move that would accomplish the basic purpose of ethnic cleansing—the removal of all non-Serbs from the region. Prominent non-Serbs who weren't getting the hint that they were supposed to leave Banja Luka were sometimes killed in the streets or would simply disappear, never to be heard from again. The Bosnian Serb leadership generally blamed such incidents on "rogue elements."

Ordinary Bosnian Serbs were witness to the acts of ethnic cleansing perpetrated by Bosnian Serb forces. In many cases, the victims were their neighbors and friends. But while some attempted to stop ethnic cleansing, other Bosnian Serbs supported it and even participated in it. Bosnian Serb leaders gathered public support by broadcasting a steady stream of **propaganda** stating that Bosnian Muslims and Bosnian Croats were killing, brutalizing, and oppressing Serbs elsewhere in Bosnia and that all actions against these groups were taken in self-defense. This type of media manipulation enabled the Bosnian Serb leadership to justify ethnic cleansing.

Through these methods, Bosnian Serb forces rid Banja Luka and other towns and villages of their entire non-Serb populations. It was estimated that during the summer of 1992, Bosnian Serb forces removed more than one million Bosnian Croats and Bosnian Muslims from their homes. The refugees created by these ethnic cleansing operations fled either into Croatia or into the areas of Bosnia still controlled by the Bosnian government.

British and U.S. journalists also revealed in the summer of 1992 that the Bosnian Serbs had detained in camps nearly 170,000 Bosnian Mus-

Bosnian refugees set up makeshift housing in a train in the Croatian town of Cacovetc. In the early months of the war, Bosnian Serb forces packed some of the victims of ethnic cleansing onto trains and sent them to Croatia. Other refugees fled to areas of Bosnia controlled by the Bosnian government.

© Kodia Photo & Graphics

The Camps

In the summer of 1992, U.S. and British reporters covering the Bosnian war revealed the existence of detention centers where Bosnian Serbs were holding captured Bosnian Muslims and Bosnian Croats. Interviews with survivors of the Omarska camp, in northwestern Bosnia, portrayed the camp as a place where prisoners were starved, beaten, and killed. In his book *Seasons in Hell,* British journalist Ed Vulliamy described a shedlike building at the Omarska camp:

"The taking of careful evidence reveals Omarska to have been a place of savage killing, torture, humiliation and barbarous cruelty... Men would be kept in the shed to await interrogation. After being 'interviewed' with the help of torture, those deemed to have been part of the resistance were then sent to the 'White House'..., which meant certain death, usually by beating or stabbing. Only five men seem to have survived it."

Inmates at the Trnopolje camp

The Bosnian Serb authorities insisted that all the detained individuals were soldiers. But in addition to Omarska, reporters also discovered that the Bosnian Serbs were running other camps where they detained and tortured civilians. The Bosnian Serb authorities eventually let the International Red Cross and the news media inspect the Omarska camp, but by then they had dispersed the prisoners to other sites in Bosnia.

The Bosnian Serbs were not the only group to detain civilians during the war. The Bosnian Croats also organized camps for captured Bosnian Muslims, subjecting them to torture and abuse. All sides in the war routinely detained civilians to use in prisoner of war exchanges or for goods such as fuel, food, and alcohol.

lims and Bosnian Croats. While some of those detained were combatants in the war, many were civilians who had been forced from their homes. The journalists revealed that most of the inmates were starving, many were beaten and tortured, and some were executed. In the case of several camps established for the detention of young girls and women, Bosnian Serb militiamen repeatedly raped the prisoners. The Bosnian Serb leadership continually denied these allegations and claimed that Bosnian Muslims and Bosnian Croats were running their own camps for Bosnian Serb prisoners.

The parliament building in Sarajevo went up in flames after being hit by a Bosnian Serb artillery shell in August 1992. Throughout the war, Bosnian Serb forces bombarded the capital city with heavy gunfire.

THE SIEGE OF SARAJEVO

In addition to ethnic cleansing, the most famous element of the war in Bosnia was the long siege of Sarajevo, the capital of Bosnia. Sarajevo, where members of all three ethnic groups made their homes, was surrounded by Bosnian Serb forces very early in the war. During most of this time, intermittent shelling with heavy artillery pummeled the city. Meanwhile, Bosnian Serb snipers (people who shoot from a hidden position) would take shots at innocent civilians from the hills around the city. In May of 1992, Bosnian Serb artillery gunners hit a Sarajevo maternity clinic, setting ablaze a building in which 70 pregnant women and 173 babies were sleeping. In the same month in the same city, mortar fire rained down on a market area where men, women, and children had lined up to get bread. The attack killed 20 and injured more than 160 people. Bosnian Serb gunners would launch similar attacks on the city throughout the war.

Bosnian Serb forces unleashed a similar encirclement and bombardment upon several other cities, including Tuzla, Gorazde, Srebrenica, Zepa, and Bihac. Before the war, these Bosnian cities had largely Muslim populations and were surrounded by countryside with mostly Serb populations. But refugees from ethnic cleansing operations began fleeing by the tens and even hundreds of thousands into these cities starting in 1992. The results were cities with far more people than they could house or feed, enduring intermittent bombardments and occasional direct attacks. Civilians in these cities had to live off humanitarian aid brought in by the United Nations (UN).

The Siege of Sarajevo

The siege of Sarajevo was one of the never ending stories of the Bosnian war. As the months wore on, the siege became such a fixture that it took a major bloodbath to attract much attention. Television alone could not convey the kind of conditions that residents of Sarajevo (*below*) faced. Daily life in Sarajevo became a game of chance, in which any trip to school, to work, or to a store might attract the fatal attention of a sniper or might lead into the path of a mortar shell. But this was a chance most Sarajevans had to take. In this once-prosperous city, food, water, heat, medical supplies, and most other necessities of life were in perpetually short supply.

American journalist David Rieff wrote that: "Ordinary people found themselves facing circumstances which nothing in their education or past experience had given them any basis for coping with . . . People who had never been cold except on the ski slope were suddenly cold for months at a time. People who had bathed twice a day had to get used to taking cold cat baths a few times a month. . . . People who had prided themselves on their honesty found themselves cutting corners to get by."

Despite these conditions, many residents of Sarajevo refused to give in to the ethnic hatred that gripped the rest of the republic. Neighbors shared food, wood, and supplies with other neighbors, regardless of their ethnicity. As much as it was possible, the people of Sarajevo tried to maintain the semblance of a normal life. The courage of Sarajevans during the siege provided a powerful image of human dignity in the face of destruction.

© Andree Kaiser/G.A.F.F. Photo Archive

The Bosnian Serbs, however, were not the only group to aggressively pursue an ethnic carveup of the republic. In early 1993, the Bosnian Croats, who had been allied with the Bosnian government, also began claiming territory to create a purely Croatian area in Bosnia. Bosnian Croat forces drove Bosnian Muslims out of the city of Mostar and committed numerous atrocities against Bosnian Muslims in other communities. In the predominantly Muslim village of Stupni Do, Bosnian Croat paramilitaries killed 25 people, torched all 52 houses, and dynamited a mosque. Bosnian Croats opened their own detention camps for captured Bosnian Muslims.

Bosnian Muslims retaliated by trying to oust Bosnian Serbs and Bosnian Croats from the few areas the Bosnian army still controlled. Soldiers fighting with the Bosnian army also committed atrocities against Bosnian Serb and Bosnian Croat civilians. Throughout the war, UN observers claimed that all parties in the war were violating human rights and committing war crimes. The victims were often innocent civilians.

FOUR TYPES OF WAR

The violence that engulfed Bosnia caught the attention of the entire world. The amount of suffering inflicted on the Bosnian people seemed to be beyond humanity. To many people, the war appeared senseless. But the Bosnian war, like many other ethnic conflicts, has origins that help to explain the reasons for the fighting.

> From the war's beginning, the national extremists who instigated the conflict aimed to destroy Bosnia as a pluralistic state and extinguish the dream of mutual tolerance.

The conflict in Bosnia could be called a war about secession. The Bosnian Serbs wanted to secede from the rest of Bosnia and they declared their independence in 1992. The Bosnian Croats, at times, said they also wanted to secede from Bosnia to form a tiny state of their own. The government of Bosnia, led by Bosnian Muslim president Alija Izetbegovic, desired to preserve Bosnia as a multiethnic country within its internationally recognized borders. So one of the primary questions that the conflict was meant to settle was whether the Bosnian Serbs (and perhaps the Bosnian Croats as well) would be able to secede from Bosnia.

In appealing to the world on behalf of its cause, the Bosnian government asserted the right—which all nations claim—to defend the integrity of its borders. The Bosnian Serbs point out that they were not the initiators of a secession movement, but rather, its victims. They weren't interested in seceding from Bosnia, they claim, until Bosnia seceded from Yugoslavia. If Bosnia could secede from Yugoslavia, they argued, why not Serbs from Bosnia? The Bosnian Serbs also argued that the numerical superiority of the Bosnian Muslims would make them a vulnerable minority in the republic.

Nevertheless, the United States, the European Community (EC, which in 1993 was renamed the EU), and the UN recognized the independence of Bosnia, a move that meant they accepted Bosnia's secession. In searching for a solution to the war, most of the outside parties—and, of course, the Bosnian government—insisted that the final settlement must preserve the status of Bosnia as a single country.

The Bosnian war can also be viewed as a war about ethnicity. The war was fought among armies that are most easily understood as representing the Bosnian Serbs, the Bosnian Croats, and the Bosnian Muslims. To outsiders, the conflict appeared to be a war in which Bosnia's Muslims, Croats, and Serbs were fighting one another out of sheer hatred. Although this simplifies the issue, ethnicity was a significant element of the Bosnian war. Two combatants in the war, the Bosnian Serbs and the Bosnian Croats, pursued a division of Bosnia based on ethnic grounds.

In many wars, ethnic conflict leads to the most brutal conduct. But the ethnic cleansing operations of the Bosnian war held a special power to shock the world because they happened in Europe and conjured up memories of World War II,

© Andree Kaiser/G.A.F. Photo Archive

A Bosnian woman rushes her injured child to safety. Approximately 17,000 children were killed over the course of the war.

A member of the Bosnian army takes aim from the ruins of a building in Sarajevo. Many soldiers in the Bosnian army— which was made up mostly of Bosnian Muslims but also included Bosnian Serbs and Bosnian Croats—had little or no military training prior to the war.

Reuters/Corbis-Bettmann

when the Nazis tried to justify the killing and oppression of millions of people on explicitly religious and ethnic grounds.

It should be noted that the Bosnian government and army, which were comprised mostly of Bosnian Muslims, did not like to be called the "Muslim government" or the "Muslim army"—as they often were in U.S. and European press accounts. Both the government and army included Serbs and Croats among their numbers. Although Muslim-dominated,

they fought to maintain a multiethnic Bosnia.

But the idea of avoiding an ethnic division of Bosnia was lost early in the war. All proposed peace settlements assumed that Bosnia would be divided among its ethnic groups. The question remained whether the ethnic regions would be required to coexist within a loose federal structure. If so, a pretense of a multiethnic Bosnia might be preserved and the outside world could say that an outright secession by the Bosnian Serbs was avoided.

After 1993 the fighting in Bosnia was about where the borders would be drawn between those ethnic regions. As much as they might have claimed that they were fighting against an ethnic division of their country, the government and army of Bosnia were forced by circumstances to fight for as big a slice of land for Bosnian Muslims as they could gain by means of war or diplomacy.

Many wars are, at some level, about efforts by the strong to expand their territory at the expense of the weak. Bosnia's war can be categorized as a territorial war because of the roles played by Bosnia's neighboring republics, Serbia and Croatia.

Serbian nationalists have long harbored a belief that Serbia's official territory is smaller than it should be, given that ethnic Serbs form a majority of the population in many areas of Bosnia and Croatia. They have envisioned re-creating what they sometimes call "greater Serbia" by absorbing the areas of Croatia and Bosnia in which ethnic Serbs predominate. Serbian president Slobodan Milosevic, a politician who used Serbian nationalism to gain political power, has supported these feelings. In the early 1990s, if not before, many of the ethnic Serbs of Croatia and Bosnia became interested in linking up with their ethnic homeland.

The war in Bosnia can be viewed as part of the effort to make that vision a reality. In 1992 Serbia had a promising opportunity to expand its borders at the expense of Bosnia. It was widely believed that at the beginning of the Bosnian war, the Serbian government

> *"Average people didn't start the war . . . we just had to fight in it."*

and JNA troops were directly involved on the side of the Bosnian Serbs, supporting their efforts with weapons and supplies so that the Republika Srpska could secede from Bosnia and eventually join Serbia.

The territorial ambitions of Croatian nationalists were also a factor in the Bosnian war. Croatia is a wealthy region, compared with either Serbia or Bosnia. It has important allies in Europe and is not landlocked, as Bosnia is. In addition, Croatian president Franjo Tudjman has actively supported Croatian nationalism. During the Bosnian war, Bosnian Croats had their own paramilitary forces, the Croatian Defense Council (HVO), which Croatia armed and aided.

The Bosnian Croats played a shifting role during the conflict, sometimes allying with the Bosnian Muslims against the Bosnian Serbs, sometimes trying to get as much territory as possible under their control to form their own ministate. Like the Bosnian Serbs, many Bosnian Croats ultimately wanted to join with their ethnic homeland to form a "greater Croatia." In fact, it was widely believed that before the war, Tudjman and Milosevic conspired to divide Bosnia between them.

One more way to view the Bosnian conflict is as a war about historic grudges. Through a complex set of historical circumstances, Serbs, Croats, and Muslims came to share the small republic known as Bosnia. During the past 500 years, however, these groups have been involved in numerous conflicts with one another. These conflicts have led to grudges that have made the Balkans an unstable region for most of the twentieth century.

CHAPTER 1   *The Recent Conflict and Its Effects*

2

THE CONFLICT'S ROOTS

In the last centuries B.C., a group known as the Illyrians became the first civilization to make a lasting mark on the territory that would become Bosnia. The Illyrians were mostly herders and warriors who occasionally traded with Greek merchants along the Adriatic coast. Eventually Celtic peoples invaded the region, creating a mixed Celtic-Illyrian culture noted for its pottery, jewelry, and iron tools.

During the first century A.D., the area came under the control of the Roman Empire. The Romans brought order, introduced their culture (including the Latin language), and developed urban areas by building roads, water systems, and forums. By the fourth century A.D., the Roman Empire had embraced the Christian faith, which spread throughout Europe. The pope be-

came the leader of the empire's Christians. Meanwhile, the Romans divided their empire into a western half, with its capital in Rome, and an eastern half, with its headquarters in Constantinople (modern Istanbul, Turkey). The eastern branch became known as the Byzantine Empire.

A stone fortress started by the Romans still stands in Banja Luka, in northwestern Bosnia.

THE SLAVIC PEOPLES

Part of the administrative border between the eastern and western sections of the empire meandered through lands that would eventually be inhabited by the ancestors of Serbs, Croats, Slovenes, Montenegrins, and Macedonians. These peoples, who were known as the South

Slavs, settled in the Balkans in the sixth and seventh centuries A.D. They spoke an Indo-European language and organized themselves into clans. Eventually, the South Slavs broke into groups and settled in different parts of the region.

The Croats settled west of the imperial dividing line, occupying an area that corresponds to modern Croatia and most of present-day Bosnia. They looked west to Rome for leadership. Their Serbian cousins conquered and settled in the regions that make up what would become southern Serbia, Montenegro, and Herzegovina. These regions happened to be east of the imperial boundary and therefore were under the influence of Constantinople.

In 1054 arguments between the popes in Rome and the emperors in Constantinople over the proper practice of Christianity eventually led to a schism—a division of the Christian world between westerners, who became Roman Catholics, and easterners, who became Orthodox Christians. Again the dividing line ran between Serbia

In the early 1200s, Stefan Nemanja united the Serbs and created an independent Serbian state. His family ruled Serbia for the next 200 years.

and Croatia. Croats followed the western form of Christianity, while the Serbs practiced the eastern variant. These religious connections helped create a tendency for modern Croats to view themselves as part of the western world and modern Serbs to view themselves as part of the Orthodox world.

COMPETING CLAIMS FOR BOSNIA

In the centuries after their arrival in the Balkans, Serbia and Croatia both experienced a golden age when each was the dominant

Balkan power and when each controlled Bosnia. Croatia's golden age took place in the mid-900s under King Tomislav, whom Pope John X had crowned in 925. The Croatian Empire stretched from the Adriatic coast into Serbia and included most of Slovenia and Bosnia. But by the next century, Croatia was subdued by Hungary, its larger neighbor to the north. The relationship between Hungary and Croatia ranged from periods when it could be called an alliance to periods when Croatia could be said to be under Hungarian domination.

Serbia, which had developed into a principality under the Byzantine Empire, became an independent state in the early thirteenth century. The Serbian golden age came in the mid-1300s under Stefan Dusan, when Serbia controlled territories that would become part or all of Bosnia, Montenegro, Albania, Greece, Macedonia, and Bulgaria. During this period, Serbia was the most powerful kingdom in the Balkan region.

From this history emerged a tendency for Serbian nationalists to think of the Bosnian region as rightfully part of their ancestral homeland while Croatian nationalists think of it as part of theirs. When a chaotic period throws the border questions open, or when Serbian or Croatian power surges, nationalists in both countries dust off their memories of the golden age and reassert their claim to a former territory.

During these periods, a mixture of Slavic peoples, some Catholics and some Orthodox Christians, inhabited Bosnia. They showed little loyalty to either Serbia or Croatia. When not under the authority of one of its neighbors, Bosnia enjoyed periods of independence under three rulers—Kulin, Stefan Kotromanic, and Stefan Tvrtko. In the 1100s—between the periods of maximum Croatian and Serbian power—the independent kingdom of Bosnia controlled parts of Serbia and Croatia. In 1326 the Bosnian leader Stefan Kotromanic annexed most of Herzegovina, making Bosnia and Herzegovina a single political unit for the first time. Under his nephew Stefan Tvrtko, the Bosnian kingdom grew to include Dalmatia, a section of modern–day Croa-

tia that runs along the Adriatic coast, as well as parts of northern Croatia. Turtko also had himself crowned as king of Serbia.

THE OTTOMAN OCCUPATION

The situation in Serbia, Croatia, and Bosnia changed dramatically in the fourteenth century, when the Ottoman Turks invaded the Balkans. Originally from Central Asia, the Ottoman Turks eventually took over large parts of the Middle East, North Africa, and southern Europe. They ran their vast empire from Constantinople, which they renamed Istanbul. After conquering Greece and Bulgaria, the Ottomans moved towards Serbia, which they invaded in 1389. The armies of the Ottoman Empire not only wanted to gain territory for the Turkish sultans (rulers), they also sought converts to their faith— Islam. The struggle for Serbia climaxed in 1389 with the Battle of Kosovo, when an outnumbered Serbian army

led by Prince Lazar suffered disastrous losses. News of the defeat spread throughout Europe. Although the Ottomans won the battle, they did not completely conquer Serbia until 1459.

Ottoman rule in Serbia was oppressive. Ottoman soldiers took Serbian boys from their families and brought them to Istanbul, where they were converted to Islam and were trained as troops. The Ottomans also killed Serbian nobles, took land away from the Serbian church, and cut off Serbian contact with other European countries. As a result of Turkish policies, many Serbs fled to Croatia, Bosnia, Montenegro, and Hungary.

After the conquest of Serbia, the Ottoman Empire continued its takeover of the Balkans, conquering Bosnia in 1463 and Herzegovina in 1483, with far less resistance than it had encountered in Serbia. When the Ottoman Turks conquered a non-Muslim people, they did not force everyone to convert to

Social and economic life in Serbia changed radically under the absolute rule of the Turkish sultan.

The Battle of Kosovo

Serbian tradition features the Battle of Kosovo and the ill-fated Prince Lazar as symbols of a martyred nation. According to a Serbian myth, on the eve of battle an angel offered Prince Lazar a choice between an earthly kingdom (the power to beat the Turks) or a heavenly one (the opportunity to sacrifice everything for Serbian honor and for Christianity). Lazar chose to make the sacrifice, fighting to the last soldier and giving his own life in the battle.

Serbian nationalists believe that the Christian world has never appreciated what their ancestors sacrificed at Kosovo. The nearly 500 years of Ottoman rule transformed this feeling into a belief that no one cares about the Serbs except the Serbs. They feel that they must follow their own counsel, must stand up for God and country regardless of the consequences or of outside opinion, and must be ready to embrace martyrdom as Prince Lazar did. Serbian nationalists have also used this history to implant among ordinary Serbs a hatred of Islam and a dread of being forced to live under Muslim control.

The Battle of Kosovo took place at Kosovo Polje, the Field of Blackbirds. Rather than surrender, Prince Lazar chose to fight to the death.

Islam. But they did impose harsh taxes on their Christian subjects—taxes from which Muslims were exempt—and granted social and political preferences to Muslims. The most significant benefit that Muslims received was ownership of land, on which Christian peasants were forced to work.

In Serbia these benefits never produced a large number of converts. Most Serbs retained their Orthodox Christian faith and were allowed to practice it, but they had to pay the tax and were treated as second-class subjects. In Bosnia, however, most of the nobility and many peasants converted to Islam. By the late 1500s, more than half of the population of Bosnia had converted to Islam.

During the Ottoman occupation, Bosnia absorbed the flavor of Ottoman culture. Mosques and other Turkish-style structures marked the landscape. People bought and sold goods in Turkish-style bazaars (markets), and children were educated in Islamic schools. Bosnia became the most visible symbol of Ottoman rule in the Balkans.

Built in the 1500s by the Ottomans, this bridge on the Drina River is one of the many reminders of Ottoman rule in Bosnia.

© Russell Gordon/Zuma Press Inc.

The Bogomils

During the 1200s and 1300s, Bosnia was one of the regions where a variant of Christianity called Bogomilism, which the world has since forgotten, took hold. Bogomils believed in Jesus but questioned the holiness of Mary, rejected the crucifixion, opposed any kind of religious hierarchy, and believed that Satan and God had equal powers. Roman Catholics and Orthodox Christians considered Bogomilism to be heresy (contrary to church beliefs). Hungary led a Catholic holy war in Bosnia to exterminate Bogomilism in the 1200s, but many Bosnians continued this religious practice.

The presence of Bogomils in Bosnia, however, is widely debated. Some historians believe that the actual number of real Bogomil believers in Bosnia was overstated and that the importance of the Bogomil chapter has been overrated. These historians believe that the Bosnians weren't Bogomils but were merely practicing a form of folk Christianity that the Catholic and Orthodox churches deemed heretical. Others feel that the beliefs of the Bogomils were as close to Islam as they were to Catholicism or to Orthodoxy and that this might explain why many Bosnians converted to Islam after the Ottoman Turks introduced the faith.

OTTOMANS AND HAPSBURGS

While the Turks were making their way through the Balkans, the Hapsburgs, an Austrian family, had gained control of Hungary and Croatia. To protect themselves from the Ottoman armies that had seized the eastern third of Hungary and parts of Croatia, Hungarian and Croatian nobles elected Hapsburg ruler Ferdinand I to be king of both countries. By 1587 a dividing line along the Sava River—which serves as the current border between Serbia and Croatia—separated the Hapsburg Empire from the Ottoman Empire in southern Europe. Most of Croatia and all of Slovenia were on the western side of the line while Serbia, Bosnia, Montenegro, and Macedonia were on the eastern side.

To secure their border with the Ottoman Empire, the Hapsburg Empire established the Military Frontier, an official military buffer zone that ran through eastern Croatia and Vojvodina. They encouraged Serbs fleeing the Turks to settle there. The Hapsburgs armed and subsidized the residents of the Military Frontier on the condition that they stand ready to repel any sudden westward push by the Turks. The offer attracted thousands of Serbs to the region, where they were given local independence and allowed to worship as Orthodox Christians.

Over the next two centuries, the Ottoman Turks struggled with a number of challenges from the Hapsburgs and other European powers. The Ottoman grip on the region remained strong, but many of the local rulers assigned by the empire were corrupt, which spurred local opposition. In addition, the cost of maintaining armies in the conquered areas was high. By the seventeenth century,

the empire started to weaken and Christian European nations attacked. The Ottomans lost territory in Hungary and Croatia to Christian forces. Muslims from these areas withdrew into Bosnia, thereby increasing Bosnia's Muslim population.

THE EMERGENCE OF YUGOSLAVISM

By the early 1800s, the Balkans were becoming increasingly unstable as the Ottoman Empire's grip on the region continued to wither. The Serbs, who had never lost their desire for autonomy (self-rule), pushed for independence and an end to corrupt Turkish rule. A growing sense of Serbian nationalism triggered violent uprisings in which Serbs targeted Slavic Muslims. The Turks, in response, enlisted Muslims to suppress these uprisings. Eventually, these rebellions enabled Serbia to gain a certain degree of autonomy under the Turks. In 1830 the Ottoman Empire recognized Serbia as a principality under Turkish control.

Croatia, meanwhile, struggled under the domination of the Hapsburg Empire. In 1868 the dual monarchy of

Austria-Hungary granted Croatia the authority to handle internal matters, but refused to give the Croats complete independence. In Bosnia, which was still under Ottoman control, clashes between Muslim landlords and the Christian peasantry over higher taxes had heightened ethnic tensions. When the peasantry revolted against these taxes, Bosnia's Muslims retaliated violently. Muslim suppression of the revolts led many Christian peasants to flee to Serbia and Croatia.

As the Slavic regions began to assert their identities, a movement for Slavic unity developed in Serbia and Croatia. Both the Serbs and the Croats came to see themselves as ordained to lead the liberation and unification of all of the southern Slavic groups, a sentiment that came to be known as Yugoslavism (South Slavism). At the same time, some Russian nationalists were adopting a similar ideology—called Pan-Slavism—which called for the Slavs of the Ottoman and Hapsburg Empires to throw off their various imperial yokes and take over world leadership from Turkey and

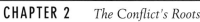

Austria-Hungary. The leader of the Slavs, presumably, would end up being the biggest and strongest Slavic nation—Russia.

Pan-Slavists and Yugoslavists may have disagreed about who was to lead the Slavic march to world leadership, but the similarity of the two ideologies created a bond between Serbia and Russia. The two nations had in common their Slavic heitage, their Orthodox Christian tradition, and their mistrust of Europe. They even used the same alphabet. And they agreed that the domination of Slavic regions by non-Slavs must end.

Yugoslavism and Pan-Slavism provided a spark to what was already a volatile area. In 1875 a revolt by Christian peasants in Bosnia against Muslim landlords led Serbia and Montenegro to declare war on the Ottoman Empire. In 1877 Russian forces joined the Serbs and Montenegrins, and the combined forces defeated the Turks in a brief war that resulted also in the liberation of Bosnia. But at the Congress of Berlin in 1878, the Great Powers—Britain, France, and Germany— established a treaty that

Religion, Ethnicity, and Nationalism

During Ottoman rule, most Bosnians identified themselves by their religious group—Muslim, Orthodox Christian, or Roman Catholic. Over time, these religious affiliations developed into cultural identities, with each group defining itself by its religious and cultural practices. Despite these differences, each group considered itself Bosnian. It was not until the development of Serbian and Croatian nationalism in the 1800s that this changed. Once Serbian and Croatian nationalists began to connect nationality with religion, Orthodox Christians in Bosnia began to identify themselves as Serbs, while Bosnian Catholics came to view themselves Croats. During the decades of Austro-Hungarian rule in Bosnia, Serbian and Croatian nationalists worked to strengthen these national connections.

The strengthening of ethnic nationalism among Christians in Bosnia was part of an effort by Serbian and Croatian nationalists to lay claim to Bosnia. This effort included the conversion of Bosnian Muslims. Each side wanted to be able to claim that Bosnian Muslims were *really* Serbs or Croats. To achieve numerical superiority, both groups encouraged Muslims to convert to Orthodox Christianity or Roman Catholicism and declare themselves Serbs or Croats. Although some Muslims did convert, most Bosnian Muslims maintained their identity. But the formation of national identities would become a permanent characteristic of Bosnian society.

redrew the spheres of influence in the Balkans. Although under the Treaty of Berlin Serbia gained independence and some additional territory, Serb nationalists were furious that the Great Powers awarded Bosnia-Herzegovina to Austria-Hungary. Slavic Muslims, who resented the Turkish withdrawal from the Balkans, also opposed the decision. Despite fierce resistance, Austro-Hungarian forces quickly conquered Bosnia.

THE ANNEXATION OF BOSNIA
Otto von Bismarck, the late-nineteenth century German

After the Treaty of Berlin was signed in 1878, Bosnian Muslims and Bosnian Serbs organized guerrilla resistance to Austro-Hungarian forces. Ultimately, however, Austria-Hungary was able to conquer and pacify Bosnia.

tried to create a Bosnian identity among Muslims, who were considered least attracted to Pan-Slavic impulses. The Hapsburgs also discouraged expressions of ethnic identity among Serbs and Croats and policed Bosnia closely. But these policies could not prevent the forces of nationalism and Yugoslavism from permeating the country.

During the decades of Austro-Hungarian rule in Bosnia, many Bosnian Serbs became committed to union with Serbia. A network of Orthodox priests and schoolteachers helped to strengthen Serbian nationalism among the Bosnian Serb peasantry. Serbia became even more attractive in 1903, when it introduced parliamentary democracy into a

chancellor, predicted that the next European conflict would be caused by "some damned foolish thing in the Balkans." Austro-Hungarian rule in Bosnia-Herzegovina, pitted against Yugoslavism, turned out to be the source of the foolishness. Austria-Hungary had no interest in Yugoslavism. It had millions of South Slav subjects and its own designs on Serbia. Hoping to prevent unity among the South Slavs, the Hapsburg rulers attempted to insulate Bosnia from Croatian and Serbian nationalism. Benjamin Kallay, the region's Hungarian administrator, region filled with monarchies. Two of the most famous underground organizations promoting a Bosnian union with Serbia were the Serbian Black Hand and Mlada Bosna, which means "Young Bosnia."

The Serbian Black Hand and Mlada Bosna sought every opportunity to show Austria-Hungary that they wanted to end Hapsburg rule over Bosnia. The Hapsburgs intended to demonstrate that they wouldn't be pushed out. Austria-Hungary realized its efforts to stamp out nationalism were failing and feared the possibility of Turkish attempts to reclaim Bosnia. Austria-Hungary's decision to formally annex Bosnia as a permanent possession in 1908 further enraged the Serbs.

Meanwhile, a bitter rivalry was developing between Serbs and Croats. The Croatian leadership was divided between advocates of a South Slav union and nationalists who desired to create a greater Croatia. This rivalry heated up when Austria-Hungary reincorporated the Military Frontier into Croatia, thus increasing the number of ethnic Serbs to almost 25 percent of the population. The Hungarian governor of Croatia pursued a policy of stirring up Serb-Croat resentment to prevent South Slav unity.

THE BALKAN WARS AND WORLD WAR I

Over the next few years, the Balkans were in a constant state of turmoil. In the First Balkan War of 1912–1913, Serbia, Greece, and Bulgaria combined to drive the Turks from western Macedonia, most of Albania, and a region between Macedonia and Serbia known as Kosovo. In the subsequent Treaty of London, the Serbs and the Greeks gained most of the former Ottoman lands, except Albania, which was granted independence. Conflicts arose over the division of Macedonia, however, as Bulgaria was awarded less than its leaders felt it deserved—a sentiment that led to the Second Balkan War in 1913. As a result of the two wars, Serbia doubled in size.

After years of small-scale wars, the volatile brew of ethnic nationalism and great power rivalry that was centered in the Balkans was finally coming to a boiling point. In June 1914, Archduke Franz

A Christian Orthodox priest blesses Montenegrin soldiers before the start of the First Balkan War.

Ferdinand, the heir to the Hapsburg throne, came to Sarajevo to lead military maneuvers and to ride in a parade. Gavrilo Princip, a Bosnian Serb and a member of Young Bosnia, assassinated the archduke on June 28.

Believing that the Serbian government was behind the assassination, Austria-Hungary declared war against Serbia. This marked the beginning of World War I (1914–1918). Russia rushed to defend its Serbian allies. Germany pledged to help its ally, Austria-Hungary, if the Russians got involved. France and Britain were eventually drawn into the war on the side of Russia and Serbia. Turkey joined Germany and Austria-Hungary, hoping, in return, to get back some of its former Balkan territories. The population of Bosnia, as it had been during the Hapsburg-Ottoman wars, was essentially divided between the two forces. Bosnian Serbs fought on both sides, while Bosnian Croats and Bosnian Muslims served mainly in the Austro-Hungarian forces.

Four years later, millions of people had died, and the entire European political order had been scrambled beyond

Top: *The assassination of Archduke Franz Ferdinand in Sarajevo set off World War I.* Above: *Serbian women helped to bury soldiers killed during the war. Serbia experienced heavy losses in its fight against the forces of Austria-Hungary.*

recognition or repair. World War I destroyed both the Hapsburg and Ottoman Empires, and the victorious powers created several new independent nations from former Hapsburg and Ottoman territories. (The Russian Empire also collapsed, and a Communist state called the Soviet Union replaced it.)

FORMATION OF THE SOUTH SLAV STATE

As a result of the war, the Yugoslav goal—a medium-sized state uniting the South Slav nations—became a reality in 1918. The new state was named the Kingdom of the Serbs, Croats, and Slovenes (changed to Yugoslavia in 1929), and it encompassed most of Slovenia, Croatia, Dalmatia, Montenegro, Serbia, Kosovo, Bosnia-Herzegovina, and the Serb–held areas of Macedonia. King Aleksander, a member of the Serbian royal family, ruled the new state from the Serbian capital of Belgrade. By its very name, the kingdom didn't acknowledge the existence of either a Bosnian or a Slavic Muslim nationality. The Belgrade regime considered Bosnia, Montenegro, and Macedonia to be regions of

When the South Slavic lands united to form the Kingdom of the Serbs, Croats, and Slovenes in 1918, Prince Aleksander of Serbia became king. Croatian opposition to Serbian rule was just one of the problems that plagued the new union.

southern Serbia and told the Macedonians and the Bosnian Muslims, who considered themselves distinct groups, that they were Serbs who were not sufficiently aware of the fact.

Despite achieving the goal of a South Slav state, the new country's inhabitants

> *In Serbian eyes, Yugoslavia was to be the embodiment of Serbian centralism, ruled by the Serbian dynasty and led by Serbian army officers, bureaucrats, and parliamentarians.*

were beset by fundamental differences in the areas of language and religion. By the time the kingdom was created, the Croats and other ethnic groups had developed a strong sense of nationalism. Some groups started national liberation movements that advocated independence from the kingdom. The largest political conflict was the result of Croatia's opposition to Serbian rule. While Croats advocated regional autonomy, the Serbs were bent on the idea of central rule, preferably under strong Serbian leadership.

As a result of the instability created by these political conflicts, King Aleksander abolished the constitution in 1929 and declared a royal dictatorship. His attempts to impose unity on the country's ethnic groups backfired, though, and strengthened Croatian opposition to Serbian domination. In 1931 Aleksander ended his personal rule by creating a new

constitution that provided for limited democracy, but this move failed to resolve Croatian and Serbian differences. Croatian revolutionaries paid a Macedonian to assassinate Aleksander in 1934.

After Alexander's death, his cousin Prince Pavle formed a three-man regency to rule for Alexander's son, Petar II, who was not old enough to take the throne. Pavle hoped that this new government would be able to reconcile Serbs and Croats. The new government freed political prisoners and allowed political parties to operate, but the disagreement between Croatian separatists and Serbian nationalists still remained.

Meanwhile, storm clouds were gathering around Yugoslavia as Europe headed toward the Second World War. Germany and Italy—the Axis powers—pressed the country to sign the Tripartite Pact, an agreement

to ally with those countries in case of war. With the German annexation of Austria in 1938 and the signing of the Tripartite Pact by Bulgaria and Romania, Yugoslavia was soon surrounded by enemies. The Yugoslav government relented and in March 1941 agreed to abide by the Tripartite Pact.

The signing of the pact provoked outrage in Serbia, and the resulting riots brought down the Yugoslav government and canceled adherence to the treaty. Serbs demanded that the new government fight German aggression. As a result, German ruler Adolf Hitler ordered the destruction of the Yugoslav state.

WORLD WAR II

Germany and Italy, assisted by Hungary and Bulgaria, overran and dismembered Yugoslavia in only 11 days. The aggressors immediately sliced up the spoils. Germany awarded itself part of Slovenia. Italy got the rest of Slovenia and some Adriatic coastline it had long coveted. Bulgaria regained Macedonia. And Hungary took a piece of land along its border. Bosnia-Herzegovina was awarded to Croatia.

The Axis powers entrusted the running of the enlarged Croatian state to Ante Pavelic, a Croatian nationalist and separatist who had fled to Italy during the reign of King Aleksander. Under the sponsorship of the Italian Fascist leader Benito Mussolini, Pavelic had founded the Ustasha (Insurgency) movement, which cultivated all Croatian grudges against Serbs and stirred them into a brew with hatred of Jews and Gypsies.

By 1941 Ante Pavelic's Ustasha regime was able to pursue the goal of eliminating Jews, Gypsies, and Serbs from Croatia through religious conversion, deportation, and murder. At a camp called Jasenovac, members of the Ustasha concentrated and killed thousands of Serbian men, women, and children. But the Croats were not the only group to commit acts of violence in support of the Ustasha regime. During the war, Bosnian Muslims formed a special SS unit and participated in the genocidal campaign against Serbs, Jews, and Gypsies.

Not all Croats were members of the Ustasha. Many Croats were so alienated by the movement's conduct that they risked their lives to join a resistance group known as the Partisans. Led by Josip Broz, a Communist of mixed Croatian-Slovenian background who operated under the pseudonym Tito, the Partisans took all ethnicities

Ustasha leader Ante Pavelic (left, with Italian leader Benito Mussolini) *became the head of the enlarged Croatian state when Germany overran and dismembered Yugoslavia. The methods used by the Ustasha to rid Croatia of Jews, Serbs, and Gypsies shocked even the Nazis.*

AP/World Wide Photos

In 1943 Nazi soldiers (above) *captured Partisans suspected of organizing guerrilla resistance to the Ustasha and the Axis powers. The Partisans, who were led by Josip Broz Tito* (right), *sought to free Yugoslavia and establish a Communist government.*

and all ideologies into their movement. Although many Partisans were fighting to overthrow the Ustasha and to rid Yugoslavia of the Axis forces, Tito's goal was to turn Yugoslavia into a Communist state based on the model of the Soviet Union.

Another resistance movement, this one based in Serbia and seeking the restoration of the prewar Serb monarchy, was known as the Chetniks. They were led by Draza Mihajlovic, a Serb who had been a colonel in the Yugoslav army. Although the

Partisans and the Chetniks initially cooperated, tensions soon developed over their differing goals. After the split, the Partisans and the Chetniks fought one another as fiercely as they fought the Ustasha and the Germans. Eventually the Allies threw

Young Yugoslavs give the Communist salute in 1943. After the Allies threw their support behind the Partisans, Tito was able to defeat the Ustasha, the Chetniks, and the Axis powers and unite Yugoslavia.

their support to Tito, thereby enabling the Partisans to defeat the Axis powers and the Chetniks. The argument still rages over which was the more effective movement. In Serbian legend, the Chetniks have gone down as noble commandos betrayed by the Allies. In Croatian lore, the Chetniks were Nazi collaborators.

The war claimed the lives of more than 1 million Yugoslavs, many of whom were killed by other Yugoslavs. The conflict had destroyed the country's major cities, in-dustries, and communication systems. Yugoslavia was left in chaos.

COMMUNIST YUGOSLAVIA

The Allied decision to support Tito left him in position to dominate postwar Yugoslavia. He arrested, tried, and executed thousands of Ustasha and Chetnik collaborators. He also imposed a Communist system on the reconstituted Yugoslavia. But unlike many postwar Communist leaders in eastern Europe, Tito was no puppet of the Soviet Union. He refused to take orders from Soviet leader Joseph Stalin. As a result, Stalin expelled Yugoslavia from the Cominform, an international Communist organization, in 1948. Tito removed Yugoslavia from the Soviet bloc, and for the next 40 years Yugoslavia held a curious status as the only Communist government that the United

In modern-day Bosnia, the grudges of World War II seem as fresh as yesterday's headlines. Serbs tend to refer to Croatian militia members as Ustasha, while Bosnian Croats and Bosnian Muslims refer to Bosnian Serb fighters as Chetniks. In some cases, the ethnic groups use past atrocities to justify retribution in the present—leading many people to view the current conflict as just another chapter in a long history of violence and bloodshed.

States and its western European allies didn't oppose. Alone among Communist regimes, Yugoslavia received U.S. military aid and loans from the International Monetary Fund. These loans helped Yugoslavia emerge from the destruction of World War II and become a thriving, prosperous nation.

The Yugoslavia that developed under Tito differed significantly from the Serb-dominated Yugoslavia of the post-World War I period. Tito abolished the monarchy and divided the country into six republics and two provinces that operated as a federation. In another significant move, Tito officially recognized Bosnian Muslims as a nationality, thereby giving them equal status with Croats, Serbs, Slovenes, Macedonians, and Montenegrins. Tito's Yugoslavia tried to acknowledge and respect everyone's ethnic identity, to downplay their grudges against one another, and to promote the idea that the various South Slav groups had more to unite them than to separate them. The government promoted the slogan "Brotherhood and Unity" to smooth over ethnic hatreds.

Tito's Yugoslavia was, of course, still a dictatorship. It didn't tolerate non-Comunist political parties and it limited freedom of expression. In fact, the regime made expressions of nationalism illegal and imprisoned advocates of ethnic or religious hatred. But within those limits, Yugoslavia was the most open and prosperous nation in the Communist world. In addition, it seemed to be a miracle of peaceful ethnic heterogeneity.

At a newsstand in Belgrade, the capital of the Yugoslav federation, a young Yugoslav stares at a poster of Tito. As the country's dictator, Tito was an omnipresent force in everyday life. Although Tito didn't tolerate dissent, he allowed Yugoslav citizens a freedom of movement that didn't exist in other Communist countries.

UPI/Corbis-Bettmann

While acknowledging the ethnic complexity of Yugoslavia, Tito tried hard to nurture a Yugoslav national identity. And, at times, he seemed to succeed. In Bosnia, for example, in the decades after World War II, an average of one in four marriages crossed ethnic lines. When asked their ethnicity on a census, a small but growing number of respondents during the 1960s and 1970s identified themselves as Yugoslav instead of their specific ethnicity. These developments suggested a future in which the grudges of the various South Slavs might possibly fade.

But careful observers saw evidence that tension existed. Croatia and Slovenia, the two most prosperous republics, often complained that they were paying the bills for the others. Croatian leaders also argued that Serbs dominated the federal government, and they demanded more control over Croatian affairs. The non-Serb peoples were always on the lookout for evidence that Serbs were seeking the kind of dominance they had had between the two world wars. Any-

The 1974 Constitution

One of Tito's lasting marks on Yugoslavia was the system of government he created under the 1974 constitution. Tito was well aware that Yugoslavia—with six republics and two provinces (Kosovo and Vojvodina), each with its own distinctive ethnic and political background—held the potential for instability. To enable the federation to stay together after his death, Tito devised a decentralized system in which the republics would share power.

The 1974 constitution created an eight-member rotating presidency for the post-Tito era, with one member for each republic and province. Each year a different member would serve as the president of this body. The president would run the government with the federal assembly, and the federal executive council. Government structure at the republic level was the same, with each republic and province having a parliament and a president.

The 1974 constitution established a decentralized system in which no republic had more authority than another. By granting the provinces of Vojvodina and Kosovo equal status on the federal level, the constitution specifically cut the power of Serbia—the largest and most populous republic. But the federal structure had many problems, some of which led to the eventual disintegration of Yugoslavia. Although this system allowed each republic and province to participate in federal politics on an equal level, it also gave them the power to veto central decisions. The result was that power flowed down to the republics, where it was used to promote nationalist policies that led the breakup of the federation.

thing that enhanced the power of Serbia inflamed these fears.

Meanwhile, Serbian nationalism began to grow during the 1970s. Serbs complained about the treatment of the Serbian population in Croatia and Bosnia and about the status of Kosovo and Vojvodina, two Serbian provinces where Serbs were outnumbered by other ethnic groups. Tito had given these two provinces the status of autonomous region within the Republic of Serbia, meaning that they were entitled to limited self-government. This act had angered many Serbs, who felt that these areas rightfully belonged to the Serbian nation.

Bosnia, as it had been throughout its history, became a focal point for Serbian and Croatian nationalists. Both groups argued that they were underrepresented in the Bosnian government, and some nationalist writers called openly for carving off ethnic areas of Bosnia and incorporating them into Serbia and Croatia.

Tito took occasional notice of these protests and complaints, sometimes suppressing them and sometimes appeasing them. And for 35 years, his mixture of velvet glove and iron fist seemed to work. But his tactics merely bottled up the grudges that the Yugoslav nationalities harbored toward one another. It didn't take long after Tito's death in 1980 for the cork to come out of the bottle and for the contents to begin oozing forth. ⊕

Many Yugoslavs genuinely mourned the loss of the leader who had brought unity to their country. However, the unity that Tito imposed on Yugoslvia would not survive his death.

3

ENTRENCHED POSITIONS

After Tito's death in 1980, Yugosavia's central government began to weaken as the individual republics sought to gain more power within the country's federal structure. The Yugoslav system of federal government, which consisted of an eight-member rotating presidency and a legislature, prevented a strong leader from emerging and advocating a common goal. Without Tito, regional interests took precedence over federal issues. The leaders of the republics, who wielded a great deal of power, saw little use in compromising on issues of political and economic significance.

The inability of the republics to agree on economic reform was a key issue of concern. Beginning in the early 1980s, the Yugoslav economy entered a period of steep decline. Inflation skyrocketed, personal incomes and living standards fell, and unemployment grew. In addition, an inequality in the distribution of income became more apparent. These problems aggravated ethnic animosities in Yugoslavia's poorer regions. In a state that promised social equality, the economic downturn created popular resentment towards the central government.

The economic situation also highlighted tensions between the republics. Croatia and Slovenia had stronger economies that emphasized high technology, whereas the southern regions—Bosnia, Macedonia, Montenegro, Kosovo, and southern Serbia—had weak economies that relied on agriculture and textile manufacturing. Both Slovenia and Croatia were irritated that the federal government diverted their earnings into the Fund for Underdeveloped Regions, which helped subsidize industries in the poorer republics.

Facing Page:
Many European and international leaders fear that the ethnic problems that have led to the carnage in Bosnia and Croatia could spread to the other former Yugoslav republics and beyond. For example, a conflict in Macedonia—which has long been a disputed region—could potentially involve Serbia, Greece, Bulgaria, and Turkey.

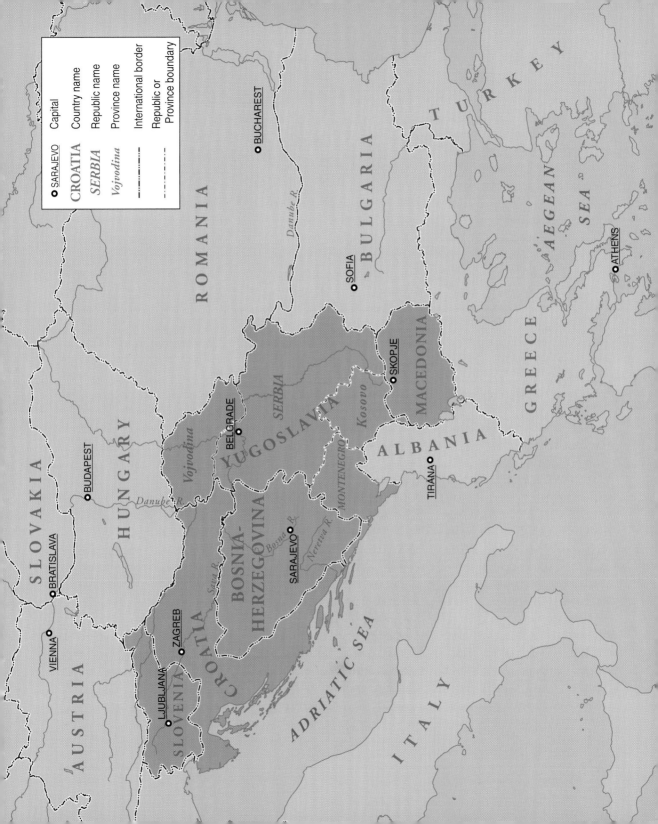

○ SARAJEVO	Capital
CROATIA	Country name
SERBIA	Republic name
Vojvodina	Province name
··············	International border
–·–·–·–·–	Republic or Province boundary

SLOVAKIA

BRATISLAVA ○

AUSTRIA

VIENNA ○

ROMANIA

BUCHAREST ○

Danube R.

BUDAPEST ○

HUNGARY

Danube R.

BULGARIA

SOFIA ○

TURKEY

AEGEAN SEA

GREECE

ATHENS ○

MACEDONIA

SKOPJE ○

Kosovo

SERBIA

Vojvodina

BELGRADE ○

YUGOSLAVIA

ALBANIA

TIRANA ○

MONTENEGRO

Sava R.

BOSNIA-
HERZEGOVINA

Bosna R.

SARAJEVO ○

Neretva R.

ZAGREB ○

CROATIA

LJUBLJANA ○

SLOVENIA

ADRIATIC SEA

ITALY

Communism's downfall further weakened the Yugoslav federation. In the late 1980s, a wave of change swept through the countries within the Soviet bloc, where opposition to Communist repression had been growing for many years. This opposition came to a head in 1989 and 1990, as protesters ousted Communist governments and introduced multiparty democracies in Poland, Czechoslovakia, Hungary, and East Germany. As this transformation was occurring, a variety of political parties began to sprout up throughout Yugoslavia to challenge the political monopoly of the League of Communists of Yugoslavia (LCY).

The dominant force in Yugoslav politics since 1945, the LCY had provided all government officials at national and republic levels. Its monopoly was broken in early 1990, when Slovenia and Croatia became the first Yugoslav republics to legalize opposition parties and to hold multiparty elections. Macedonia, Bosnia-Herzegovina, and Serbia held their own multiparty elections later in 1990. As a result of the elections, the

The decade that followed the death of Tito was a time of gradual deterioration and a period that saw ethnic hostility boiling just below the surface of Yugoslav political culture.

LCY renounced its leading role in Yugoslav politics.

THE RISE OF NATIONALISM

The economic crisis and the decline of Communism paved the way for the introduction of democracy to the Yugoslav republics. But these factors also opened the door for politicians who pursued a nationalist agenda. Take, for example, the rise to power in Serbia of Slobodan Milosevic, an ambitious and opportunistic politician who would become one of the key actors in the story of the Bosnian war. As head of the Serbian League of Communists during the 1980s, Milosevich gained popularity by emphasizing Serbian nationalism. By 1989 Milosevich had become president of Serbia, and his ascension was fueled by fiery nationalist rhetoric. In his own speeches and through his manipulation of the Serbian media, Milosevic advocated the

creation of a greater Serbia that would dominate the Yugoslav federation and encompass all Serbs in Yugoslavia.

Serbs in Kosovo, Croatia, and Bosnia reacted strongly to Milosevic's nationalist rhetoric. Because the Serbs in these regions were outnumbered by other ethnic groups, they felt vulnerable. But such an expression of Serbian nationalism also activated the fears of Yugoslavia's other nationalities that Serbia would attempt to recreate the Yugoslavia of the 1920s and 1930s, when Serbia dominated the nation and oppressed non-Serb groups.

In Croatia the death of Tito and the loosening of the Yugoslav federation created political opportunities for those who had long felt that Croatia would be better off on its own. Franjo Tudjman won the Croatian presidency with a message that combined dislike of Serbs with promises to take Croatia

Slobodan Milosevic

Slobodan Milosevic is the man most widely recognized as the instigator of the Bosnian war. An economist by training, Milosevic was always a good Communist and a Serbian Nationalist. While Tito was alive, Milosevic emphasized the Communist side of his political personality and rose to a mid-level position within the Serbian republic. But after Tito's death, Milosevic began emphasizing Serbian nationalism and invoking Serbia's ancient grievances. A cunning and opportunistic politician, Milosevic used nationalism to gain the support of a population hard hit by economic difficulties. Milosevic was especially adept at playing upon Serbian sensitivity about Kosovo, one of the two autonomous regions of Yugoslavia.

Slobodan Milosevic

Kosovo lies between the main part of Serbia and Albania. The region's population is 90 percent ethnic Albanian and about 10 percent Serbian. Because of the famous battle that occurred there in 1389 and because it was the center of the ancient Serbian kingdom, Serbs call Kosovo "the cradle of Serbian civilization." Although hardly any Serbs lived there after World War II, Serbs have always insisted on controlling a region that holds such historical and symbolic importance.

While the Albanian majority in Kosovo complained that Serbs held all the region's wealth and power, Milosevic said the danger was that the Albanians might oppress the 10 percent Serbian population of Kosovo. The Albanians of Kosovo demanded more autonomy (self-governing powers), but Milosevic did not believe Kosovo should be autonomous at all. Using the Serbian media and his own inflammatory speeches, Milosevic rallied Serbian nationalists around the cause of Kosovo and aroused resentment towards the predominantly Muslim Albanians. When Milosevic revoked Kosovo's autonomy, Serbian nationalists hailed him as a hero.

The Kosovo issue is an example of how Slobodan Milosevic became one of the most powerful leaders in the former Yugoslavia. Milosevic used historic myths and ethnic stereotypes to direct the frustrations of ordinary Serbs towards nationalism and ethnic hatred. His words and actions would later stoke the fires of ethnic hatred in Croatia and Bosnia.

back into western Europe where it belonged. Serb nationalists quickly concluded that Tudjman represented the second coming of the Ustasha. They feared he would try to suppress the 600,000 ethnic Serbs living in the Croatian Krajina, descendants of those who had participated four centuries earlier in the Hapsburg military buffer-zone arrangement.

Serbian nationalists believed that as long as Croatia remained within a Yugoslav federation in which Serbs were the strongest nation, the Serbian population in Croatia would be protected. But in an independent Croatia, the Serbs of the Krajina would have no such protection. Given the Serbian nationalist view that Croatia had fallen under the control of anti-Serb fascists, this would be an unacceptable arrangement.

WARNING SIGNS
The Yugoslav government had long advertised the harmony among Bosnia's three biggest ethnic groups. This was challenged by the results of the first-ever free elections in Bosnia, held in November of 1990. Bosnian Muslims voted a Muslim ticket, led by a scholar named Alija Izetbegovic. Bosnian Serbs gave their support to a local branch of the party headed by Slobodan Milosevic. And Bosnian Croats backed a local branch of the party led by Franjo Tudjman. Because the Bosnian Muslims were the most numerous group, Izetbegovic received the most presidential votes. Voters also elected a multiparty assembly made up of 99 Bosnian Muslims, 83 Bosnian Serbs, and 50 Bosnian

Reuters/Corbis-Bettmann

The multiparty elections held in 1990 led to the creation of a multiethnic government that was headed by Alija Izetbegovic. Like many other Bosnian Muslim politicians, Izetbegovic believed that a multiethnic state provided the best protection for Muslim interests.

Franjo Tudjman

© Robert Rajtic/Zuma Press Inc.

Franjo Tudjman

Like Slobodan Milosevic, Franjo Tudjman is credited with helping to stir up ethnic hatred in the former Yugoslavia. During his young adulthood he was a loyal Communist and became the youngest general in the JNA. During the 1970s, Croatian nationalism emerged as the dominant trait in his political personality. Like his counterpart Slobodan Milosevic, Tudjman used nationalism and media control to gain power. His desire for an independent Croatia and his anti-Serb rhetoric built him a strong following among Croatian nationalists.

Contrary to Serbian propaganda, Tudjman is no Ustasha. In fact, as a young man he fought with Tito's Partisans against the Ustasha. But like most Croatian nationalists, Tudjman tends to minimize the Ustasha genocide against the Serbs. In his autobiography, he estimated that only 40,000 Serbs were killed at Jasenovac concentration camp—an even smaller number than the traditional Croatian underestimate. To Serbs, anyone who would so minimize the Ustasha genocide must want to justify it and may seek to resume it.

Tudjman fed Serbian fears by backing a series of measures designed to force Serbs in the Republic of Croatia to use the Latin alphabet and the Croatian variant of the Serbo-Croatian language. According to Misha Glenny of the British Broadcasting Corporation, who interviewed Croatian Serbs near the city of Knin: "The move (on language and alphabet) was as senseless as it was provocative. According to moderate Knin Serbs I met in 1990, only about five percent of the local Serbs used the Cyrillic script. The rest not only spoke the Croatian variant, they used the Latin script."

Pointless as they were, such measures heightened fears about what would become of Croatia's Serbs if the republic seceded. Eventually, Tudjman's provocation of ethnic Serbs led to the Croatian war. The Croatian president's nationalist rhetoric would later provoke the Bosnian Croats to create their own ministate in Bosnia.

Croats. After the elections, President Izetbegovic formed a coalition government with a multimember presidency that allotted two spaces each to Bosnian Muslims, Bosnian Serbs, and Bosnian Croats. Although the transition to a multiparty democracy had been peaceful, the fact that Bosnians had voted along ethnic lines was an ominous sign. It showed that Bosnia's voters felt that only their ethnic kin could represent their interests.

Izetbegovic was more serious about his faith than many Bosnian Muslims. In 1970 he had written a document called the Islamic Declaration, in which he had argued that homogeneous Muslim societies should be ruled by Muslim governments. He had written the declaration for the entire Muslim world. It never mentioned Bosnia. In fact, multiethnic Bosnia—where Muslims are not an overwhelming majority, and where most Muslims are not very religious—was not the kind of society that Izetbegovic was writing about. But Serbian and Croatian propaganda claimed that Izetbegovic's declaration proved that he

Once he became the president of the Serbian Democratic Party (SDS), Radovan Karadzic called for equal cultural, religious, and economic rights for the Serbs of Bosnia.

was an Islamic fundamentalist who meant to turn Bosnia into a society like Iran, where non-Muslim rights are not always respected. Through the eyes of Serbian nationalists, the election of Izetbegovic looked like the return of the Ottoman Empire and raised the unacceptable prospect of hundreds of thousands of Bosnian Serbs living under Muslim rule.

The most vocal Bosnian Serb supporter of this point of view was Radovan Karadzic, president of the Serbian Democratic Party (SDS), which had been formed before the elections in 1990. A psychiatrist and a poet, Karadzic was also a rabid Serbian nationalist who distrusted all non-Serbian ethnic groups. He believed Serbs had a historic right to territory that no longer had a Serbian population. Karadzic would play an important role in stirring up Bosnian Serb resentment to the new government.

SECESSION
After the 1990 elections, the new leadership in Croatia and Slovenia proposed a looser confederation of the Yugoslav republics, with each republic having national sovereignty, its own army, and its own foreign policy. These impulses reflected the desire of the two republics to distance themselves from their poorer neighbors and to avoid the danger that Serbia was seeking to dominate the post-Tito Yugoslavia.

Serbia refused to go along with the confederation arrangement, claiming that this proposal would make

Serbs in the other republics foreign citizens. Slovenia and Croatia hinted strongly that they would secede from Yugoslavia if the republics couldn't produce a satisfactory agreement to decentralize power. Milosevic and the JNA, which was dominated by ethnic Serb officers, hinted just as clearly that they would not accept the dismemberment of Yugoslavia. Tensions increased in the spring of 1991, when Croatian authorities began cracking down on Croatian Serb separatists in the Krajina, who strongly opposed Croatian independence. Fearing for the safety of all Serbs in the Croatian Kra-jina, Milosevic sent in the JNA as a peacekeeping force.

By June 1991, both Croatia and Slovenia had declared their independence. That summer, the Yugoslav wars began in Slovenia—the first republic to secede. The JNA tried but failed to compel Slovenia to back down. The fighting lasted only 10 days. Slovenia had two important advantages over Croatia and later Bosnia—it had no border with Serbia and no large Serb population within the republic. Slovenia's independence was quickly recognized by the UN, the European Community (EC, which in 1993 was renamed the EU), and the United States.

The war in Croatia began in July of 1991. Supplied with weapons smuggled in from Serbia, the Croatian Serbs declared their own independence from Croatia, forming the Republic of the Serbian Krajina. The initial fighting occurred between Serbian guerrillas and Croatian militia units. Soon, however, the peacekeeping role of the JNA expanded into support for Serbian forces. Eventually, the JNA occupied parts of Croatian territory. What had begun as a peacekeeping force had turned into an instrument of Serbian aggression.

The war was short but extremely fierce. An estimated

A casualty of the Slovenian secession lies on the side of the road. The 10-day war in Slovenia produced casualties for both the Serbs and the Slovenes. JNA soldiers took up positions in Slovenia to prevent illegal secesion, but withdrew when they experienced unexpectedly stiff resistance.

© Kodia Photo & Graphics

10,000 people were killed, and about 600,000 people became refugees. By the end of the war, Serbian forces controlled almost one-third of Croatia. In November 1991, the United Nations authorized the deployment of up to 10,000 peacekeeping troops if the warring parties in Croatia could reach a cease-fire agreement. In December former U.S. Secretary of State Cyrus Vance, acting as a special UN envoy, succeeded in brokering just such a truce, which took effect in January 1992.

To help prevent the conflict from spreading to the other republics, the UN imposed a worldwide **embargo** (restriction) on arms sales and shipments to all the Yugoslav republics. In addition, the UN established the United Nations Protection Force (UNPROFOR), whose troops were deployed in areas where interethnic tensions had led to conflict. These troops would help maintain the peace in Croatia.

BOSNIA DESCENDS INTO WAR
While the fighting raged in Croatia, Bosnian president Izetbegovic saw the implications for his republic. If

Plumes of smoke rose from the historic walled Croatian city of Dubrovnik after a shelling by the JNA in November 1991. The Croatian war destroyed many historic buildings and wiped out nearly 40 percent of the country's industry.

Croatia and Slovenia seceded, the Croats and the Muslims of Bosnia would not want to remain in a Yugoslavia dominated by Serbs. But if Bosnia seceded, it would be almost defenseless against its more powerful neighbor. In 1991, therefore, Izetbegovic urged foreign governments to step in and keep Yugoslavia together. But the EU announced in December 1991 that it would recognize the independence of Croatia and Slovenia. Izetbegovic then asked that UN troops be placed in Bosnia before trouble could start, but the UN denied the request.

By that time, Bosnia was seeing the first flareups of ethnic fighting. The republic's ethnic groups had drawn distinct lines, with Bosnian Serbs wanting to remain in Yugoslavia, Bosnian Croats wanting to leave the federation, and Bosnian Muslims wishing to maintain an independent, multiethnic state. The Bosnian Serbs declared certain areas of northern and eastern Bosnia to be Serbian Autonomous Regions. Evidence suggested that Serbia was secretly delivering arms to these regions. Radovan Karadzic warned that Bos-

nian Serbs would not give up their right to remain part of Yugoslavia. Although they had different agendas, the Bosnian Muslims and Bosnian Croats both opposed the secessionist ambitions of The Bosnian Serbs.

Despite the warnings of Karadzic, the Bosnian presidency voted to petition the EU to recognize Bosnia as an independent state. The Europeans said they would do so if Bosnians chose independence in a referendum (public vote). The Bosnian government scheduled the independence referendum. But, just as Izetbegovic had feared, Bosnia's Serbs, through their leaders, said they would boycott the vote. The Bosnian Serb leadership further threatened that if Bosnia voted to secede from Yugoslavia, the Serbian Autonomous Regions would secede from Bosnia and eventually link up with Serbia.

In March of 1992, Bosnia's non-Serbs voted for independence by more than a 90-

percent majority. In response, the Bosnian Serbs declared their own independent state, Republika Srpska, whose borders encompassed the Serbian Autonomous Regions. Shortly after the vote, JNA units and Bosnian Serb paramilitary forces attacked towns in the south, west, and northwest of Bosnia. On April 6, the EU and the United States recognized Bosnia's independence. On the day of EU recognition, Bosnian Serb paramilitaries fired on a crowd of peace demonstrators in Sarajevo. The war had begun.

AN UNEVEN BATTLE

From the beginning, in military terms, the war was a rout in favor of the Bosnian Serb forces. Aided by JNA forces under the command of General Ratko Mladic, the Bosnian Serbs concentrated their assault in northern and eastern Bosnia, where they implemented ethnic cleansing. The goal of the Bosnian Serb forces was to make these areas ethnically uniform,

> *"There is no ethnic cleansing . . . but ethnic shifting. We are doing it to protect people."*
> —*Radovan Karadzic*

General Ratko Mladic

How the JNA Became a Serbian Army

Before the breakup of Yugoslavia, the Yugoslav People's Army (called the JNA under its Serbo-Croatian acronym) ranked as one of the 10 strongest armies in Europe. During the years under Communist rule, the JNA occupied a position as one of the country's most significant unifying forces. Although primarily responsible for defending the federation from external threats, the JNA also protected the state from internal divisions. Because all male citizens were subject to conscription, the JNA brought together men from all parts of Yugoslavia and all its ethnic groups.

Although all of Yugoslavia's ethnic groups were represented in the JNA, ethnic Serbs dominated the JNA officer corps and the high command. When the federation came apart in 1991, Serbia managed to control most of the JNA's arms, ammunition, and other equipment. Leading JNA officers aligned themselves with Slobodan Milosevic. The JNA then became heavily involved in Serbia's efforts to prevent secession in Slovenia and Croatia. Before the Bosnian war began, JNA troops were stationed inside the republic to protect Bosnia's Serbs from Muslim aggression.

Once the fighting in Bosnia started, the JNA provided the Bosnian Serb paramilitaries with weapons and supplies. More important, Milosevic and the JNA had devised a plan to transfer out of Bosnia all soldiers who were not Bosnian Serbs and to bring in Bosnian Serb soldiers serving in other areas of the country. Under international pressure to stop aiding Bosnian Serb aggression, Milosevic ordered the JNA to withdraw—but this order allowed soldiers from Bosnia to remain. This policy essentially created a Bosnian Serb army that had access to all the supplies and weaponry of the JNA. As a result, the Bosnian Serbs began the war with a tremendous advantage in trained personal, arms, and other military equipment.

thereby allowing them to carve out territory for Republika Srpska. Ultimately, they hoped to connect this territory to Serbia proper via the Croatian Krajina, which Serb forces had conquered in the Croatian war. Through ethnic cleansing, Bosnian Serb and JNA forces chased almost all of the Bosnian Muslims and Bosnian Croats out of captured towns and villages. By the end of April, the Bosnian Serbs had driven 286,000 non-Serbs from their homes.

Two Bosnian army soldiers in Sarajevo monitor events from their trench. Bosnian Serb forces were able to cut Sarajevo off from the rest of the world, but the resistance of the Bosnian army and militia gangs prevented the Bosnian Serbs from completely overrunning the capital.

Meanwhile, the siege of Sarajevo was just beginning. When President Izetbegovic became aware of what was happening in northern and eastern Bosnia, he issued a general mobilization of the Bosnian territorial defense. Karadzic and other Bosnian Serb leaders, who knew that only Bosnian Muslims and Bosnian Croats would join these troops, saw Izetbegovic's move as a declaration of war. Soon after, the JNA seized control of Sarajevo Airport. Within a few weeks, the Bosnian Serb forces and the JNA were bombarding the capital from the surrounding mountains.

Karadzic's plan was to partition the city into Serb, Croat, and Muslim sectors, thereby destroying Sarajevo's centuries-old tradition of ethnic harmony. The Serb-held areas would join with the newly declared Republika Srpska. Bosnian Serb forces repeatedly shelled the city, trapping Sarajevo's residents—Croats, Serbs, and Muslims alike—in a relentless assault that did not distinguish between soldier and civilian.

Although the Bosnian army had the personnel to fight the combined forces of the Bosnian Serbs and the JNA, it lacked the weaponry. A few months before the war started, Izetbegovic—in an attempt to show his peaceful intentions—had allowed the JNA to confiscate the weapons and supplies of the local defense forces. Furthermore, the UN arms embargo, which prevented the Bosnian government from obtaining weapons legally, preserved the imbalance between the Bosnian Serb forces and the Bosnian army. While the Bosnian Serbs had the advantage of JNA weapons and equipment, soldiers in the Bosnian army had to make do with whatever weapons they could get their hands on.

By the summer of 1992, the Bosnian war was well under way, with the Bosnian Serb forces firmly in control. Besieged Sarajevo was virtually cut off from the rest of the world. Throughout northern and eastern Bosnia, Bosnian Serb forces had begun to establish camps for the detainment of Bosnian Muslims and Bosnian Croats who had been driven from their homes. Meanwhile, refugees—mostly Bosnian Muslim women and children—were flooding into Croatia, telling of the horror that was occurring in Bosnia.

At this point, U.S. and European leaders realized

Residents of Sarajevo dash across an open intersection, trying to avoid Bosnian Serb sniper fire. Because of constant sniper fire and shelling, any trip outside in Sarajevo was dangerous.

that the situation in Bosnia had reached the level of an international crisis. The UN Security Council expanded UNPROFOR's mandate to include Bosnia as well as Croatia. More than 1,000 troops were sent to Sarajevo to open up the airport for the delivery of humanitarian supplies. In August, the Security Council again added to UNPROFOR's mission by including the safe delivery of humanitarian assistance throughout Bosnia. At about the same time, the Security Council also imposed economic sanctions on Serbia (which had joined with Montenegro to form a smaller Yugoslav federation) for its role in aiding the Bosnian Serb war effort. The purpose of these sanctions was to pressure the republic from arming, funding, and encouraging the Bosnian Serbs.

In August U.S. and British journalists broke the story of

the camps where Bosnian Serb forces were detaining, torturing, and killing the victims of their ethnic cleansing operations. In October the *New York Times* reported allegations of rape camps. An EU investigative team later concluded that Bosnian Serb soldiers had raped thousands of Bosnian women and girls, the majority of them Muslims. The U.S. State Department said that the atrocities committed in the campaigns of ethnic cleansing "dwarf anything seen in Europe since the Nazis."

Despite the international attention focused on them, the Bosnian Serbs continued their assault. During the summer, Bosnian Serb attacks on the eastern Bosnian city of Gorazde were stepped up. The Bosnian Serbs centered their campaign mostly in areas where Bosnian Muslims formed a significant part of the population. Through terror, intimidation, robbery, and murder, Bosnian Serb forces were able to drive all non-Serbs from these areas into Croatia and government-held territory. By the end of 1992, the United Nations High Commissioner for Refugees (UNHCR) estimated that ethnic cleansing had turned 1.7 million Bosnians into refugees.

© Andree Kaiser/G.A.F. Photo Archive

Rape victims at a refugee center in Tuzla. Rape was just one of the tactics Bosnian Serb soldiers used to terrorize non-Serbs into leaving conquered areas.

Throughout the Bosnian war, symbols of culture and religion became the targets of ethnic cleansing operations. In their attempt to cleanse towns of Bosnian Muslims and Bosnian Croats, the Bosnian Serbs destroyed mosques and Catholic churches. In Sarajevo, Bosnian Serb gunners deliberately shelled the National Library (above), which held the largest collection of Islamic manuscripts in southeastern Europe. In areas controlled by Bosnian Croats, HVO soldiers dynamited mosques and Orthodox churches.

The destruction of cultural symbols was an important element of the conflict. By cleansing areas of the enemy populations, and destroying all symbols of the enemy culture, conquering forces could proclaim that the conquered territory had always been ethnically pure.

THE MUSLIM-CROAT SPLIT

In the early months of the war, the lives and property of Bosnian Muslims and Bosnian Croats were defended by the Bosnian army, a multiethnic force that was predominantly Muslim, and the Croatian Defense Council (HVO), which was comprised mostly of Bosnian Croats and was fully armed by Croatia. The Bosnian Muslims and the Bosnian Croats were formally partners in an alliance that had been signed by Tudjman and Izetbegovic. From the beginning, however, this alliance was strained. The Bosnian Croats distrusted the Bosnian Muslims, whom they felt had aided the JNA during the Croatian war. In addition, it was widely known that Tudjman and the Bosnian Croat leadership harbored the desire to bring Bosnian Croats into a greater Croatia.

Bosnian Croats inhabited two areas of the republic. Most Bosnian Croats lived in central and northern Bosnia in communities that included Bosnian Muslims and Bosnian Serbs. In western Herzegovina, however, Bosnian Croats made up a majority of the population. When the war broke out, the Croats in

A resident of Mostar runs through the rubble of the city, which was pounded by Bosnian Serb and Bosnian Croat artillery. After their alliance with the Bosnian Muslims disintegrated in late 1992, Bosnian Croat forces began to attack Mostar and other cities that they had previously helped to defend.

© Andree Kaiser/G.A.F.F. Photo Archive

Herzegovina—armed and aided by Croatia—were able to defeat the Bosnian Serbs and to take control of a large area of western Herzegovina, including the city of Mostar. Mate Boban, the leader of the Bosnian Croats, declared this area to be the Croatian Community of Herceg-Bosna and removed all Bosnian Muslims from positions of responsibility.

The breaking point between the Bosnian Muslims and the Bosnian Croats came in October of 1992, when a conflict between the two armies erupted in the central Bosnian town of Prozor. The Bosnian Croats suddenly made peace with the Bosnian Serbs, creating an informal alliance. By early 1993, the Bosnian Croats were essentially at war with the Bosnian Muslims. HVO soldiers attacked Bosnian Muslims in some of the cities under their control and pursued a policy of ethnic cleansing similar to that of the Bosnian Serb forces. Soon the Bosnian Croats opened detainment camps for Bosnian Muslims.

The break between Bosnia's Muslims and Croats split the republic into three separate territories. Bosnian Serb forces had conquered much of northern and eastern Bosnia, while the Bosnian Croats held much of southern Bosnia (Herzegovina). The Bosnian army, which controlled territory in central Bosnia, was essentially surrounded. The Bosnian Muslims were left with a small group of enclaves in central Bosnia that were isolated from one another and were under constant attack. It looked as if the Bosnian Serbs and the Bosnian Croats would succeed in dividing the republic into separate ethnic territories.

CHAPTER

THE PRESENT CONFLICT

As it became clear that the warring parties in the Bosnian conflict were not going to find a peaceful solution on their own, international efforts to end the fighting were stepped up. At this point, the UN, the North Atlantic Treaty Organization (NATO), and the United States took on major roles in the war.

In late 1992, UN special representatives Cyrus Vance and Lord David Owen proposed a plan to settle the Bosnian war. The Vance-Owen plan divided Bosnia into 10 provinces based primarily on ethnicity. Three of the provinces would have a Bosnian Serb majority; three would have a Bosnian Muslim majority; two a Bosnian Croat majority; and one would be a Croat-Muslim mix.

The initial reaction to the Vance-Owen plan was negative. The plan allotted 42 percent of Bosnian territory

The peace plan that negotiators Cyrus Vance (left) and Lord David Owen proposed in early 1993 would have given each side in the war a share of Bosnian territory, but the proposal pleased no one. Despite pressure from Slobodan Milosevic to accept the deal, the Bosnian Serbs refused to agree to a plan that would force them to give up their military gains.

to the Serb region, a change that would have required Bosnian Serb forces to withdraw from much of the 70 percent of Bosnia they occupied. On this basis, the Bosnian Serbs opposed the plan. Izetbegovic felt that the plan essentially sanctioned ethnic cleansing, and that refugees would never be allowed to return to their homes. The only group that was happy with the Vance-Owen plan were the Bosnian Croats, whose territorial allotment under the plan would have enabled them to join Croatia.

UN peacekeeping troops outside of Sarajevo construct a wall of sandbags around their bunker. Throughout the war the Bosnian government criticized the United Nations Protection Force (UNPROFOR) for its inability to protect Bosnian civilians from attack.

© Andree Kaiser/G.A.F.F. Photo Archive

International pressure pushed the different sides toward an agreement. In the end, however, the Bosnian Serbs rejected the Vance-Owen plan, and the killing continued.

SREBRENICA AND THE SAFE AREAS

In March 1993, the world's attention suddenly was called to Srebrenica, an obscure city in eastern Bosnia. Refugees from previous ethnic cleansing operations had swollen the city's population from 10,000 to 60,000. Under sustained bombardment by the Bosnian Serbs, who had banned all aid convoys,

Srebrenica was soon unable to provide adequate medical care to the injured. In addition, the Bosnian army soldiers defending Srebrenica had run out of ammunition. Thousands of civilians, mostly Bosnian Muslims, were trapped in the city. Many were living in the street, dying of cold and hunger.

UN general Philippe Morillon of France tried to get help to those trapped in Srebrenica. After numerous negotiations with Bosnian Serb commanders, Morillon convinced the Bosnian Serbs to allow aid convoys into the city. But the Bosnian Serbs kept shelling the town and

eventually forced Morillon to agree to have UN troops disarm the soldiers defending the town. Meanwhile, the Bosnian Serbs ensured safe passage for the refugees trapped in the city. In making this deal, the UN had unwittingly helped the attackers in their larger cause—to remove the Bosnian Muslims from Srebrenica.

Meanwhile, Bosnian Serb forces continued their siege of Sarajevo and launched bombardments on two other Muslim enclaves, Bihac and Zepa. Shortly thereafter, the UN Security Council adopted a new approach to its mission in Bosnia. In May of 1993, the

Security Council declared six besieged Bosnian cities—Sarajevo, Bihac, Gorazde, Srebrenica, Tuzla, and Zepa—as safe areas for refugees. The UN's declaration ordered the Bosnian Serbs to withdraw their forces from around these areas so that humanitarian aid could be provided to the refugees. The declaration authorized UNPROFOR troops to use force to deter any attacks and called for NATO air strikes to support the troops.

Despite its intentions, the UN's safe area declaration did not protect these six cities. The Bosnian Serbs continued to besiege these areas and block all humanitarian assistance. UNPROFOR troops did not have the firepower to sufficiently protect the safe areas. The UN could feed the refugees, but it was powerless to stop their attackers. Furthermore, NATO did not launch air strikes for fear of provoking the Bosnian Serbs and endangering UN troops.

By the summer of 1993, the Bosnian government was determined to fight back. It had already faced the fact that the international community was unwilling to use

It became increasingly evident that the Western Powers viewed the Bosnian government only as the Muslim component of a tripartite partition plan. The Muslim leaders reacted at first with disappointment and, ultimately, with despair.

force against the Bosnian Serbs and that any peace plans would recognize the territorial gains of the Bosnian Serb and Bosnian Croat forces. To connect the isolated pockets still under government control, the Bosnian army swept through central Bosnia, destroying many Bosnian Croat villages in the process. In some cases, Bosnian army soldiers used ethnic cleansing tactics similar to those employed by their enemies. In the town of Uzdol, the Bosnian army killed dozens of Bosnian Croat civilians.

Although the Bosnian army regained some territory in central Bosnia, the overall situation still favored the Bosnian Serbs. Every peace plan put forward throughout the summer of 1993, like the Vance-Owen plan, divided Bosnia into ethnic zones that in effect rewarded Bosnian Serb aggression. President

Izetbegovic and the Bosnian government held out hope that NATO would launch air strikes against the Bosnian Serbs, but the NATO powers were at odds over the use of force. The United States wanted NATO air strikes to lift the siege of Sarajevo, but the British and the French—who had troops among the UN peacekeeping forces—did not. Furthermore, the UN Security Council opposed lifting the weapons ban that was handicapping the Bosnian army. The inability of the international community to end the war angered many Bosnians.

As a result, the situation in Bosnia remained unresolved throughout 1993. A couple of counteroffensives by the Bosnian army succeeded briefly, but the ground gained was usually lost in the next round of fighting. The UN, the EU, and the United States made a lot of threats

Much of the media coverage during the war focused on the behavior of the Bosnian Serb and the Bosnian Croat forces, but the Muslim-dominated Bosnian army also committed war crimes and participated in ethnic cleansing. A Bosnian Serb woman (left) holds the skull of her son, killed by the Bosnian army and buried in a mass grave. In June 1993, UN soldiers (below) had to evacuate Bosnian Croats from Guca Gora as the Bosnian army advanced on the town.

Reuters/Corbis-Bettmann

to use force, followed through on few, and proposed several settlements to end the war. The UN established an international war crimes tribunal to investigate war crimes and atrocities. Cease-fires were declared and broken as the fighting continued, with the conflict between Bosnian Muslims and Bosnian Croats growing more intense. Meanwhile, the Bosnian Serbs continued to attack besieged cities and safe areas, where food was scarce. The trapped civilians were slowly being starved to death.

Reuters/Corbis-Bettmann

SOME PROGRESS

The international ambivalence about military involvement in the Bosnian war finally changed on February 5, 1994, when a Bosnian Serb mortar landed in a crowded marketplace in Sarajevo, killing 68 and wounding more than 200. Television coverage of the attack outraged the world. Shocked by the mortar attack—which produced the biggest fatality count from any such incident during the war—NATO and the UN gave the Bosnian Serbs an ultimatum. Unless they stopped shelling Sarajevo and pulled their heavy weapons out of range or turned them over to the UN, NATO planes would attack Bosnian Serb positions surrounding the city.

At this point, Russia—Serbia's traditional ally—greatly increased its involvement in the crisis, sending 800 peacekeepers to join the UN forces. The Bosnian Serb fighters greeted the Russians as long lost family members. Their arrival relieved the Bosnian Serb feeling that they hadn't a friend left in the world. The Bosnian Serbs pulled most of their heavy

In February 1994, volunteers removed victims of the market square bombing in Sarajevo. Although world opinion assigned blame for the shelling to Bosnian Serb forces, the Bosnian Serb leadership claimed that the Bosnian government engineered the attack to persuade the international community to intervene on its behalf.

weapons away from Sarajevo and turned the rest over to the UN. NATO didn't have to bomb, the two-year siege of Sarajevo appeared over, and the UN seemed to have done something to actually end the fighting instead of just feeding the refugees. When the bombardment stopped, residents of Sarajevo returned to the streets, and businesses began to reopen.

This success was followed by another positive sign. Before the end of February, the Bosnian government and the Croatian government, which was representing the Bosnian Croats, agreed to a truce. U.S. and European diplomats were able to convince the Bosnian government and the Bosnian Croats that a truce was in their best interests. For the Bosnian government, the truce meant that the isolated Bosnian Muslim enclaves would be able to receive aid and weapons. For Tudjman and the Croats, the truce enabled them to avoid isolation within the international community for supplying weapons and soldiers to the Bosnian Croats.

In early March, as a sign of further progress, the Bosnian government and the Bosnian Croats announced an agreement to form a small economic confederation, called the Federation of Bosnia and Herzegovina, to which Croatia would also belong. This deal created the possibility of a Bosnian Muslim-Bosnian Croat coalition that could hold its own against the Bosnian Serbs.

RENEWED HOSTILITIES

The feeling that the war was close to ending soon faded. The Bosnian Serb leadership was not easily deterred by the threat of international force. As if to test the new resolve of the UN and NATO, the Bosnian Serbs launched a large-scale artillery and infantry assault on Gorazde, a government-held city 35 miles southeast of Sarajevo. The city's temporary population of 65,000 included about 40,000 refugees. Although it was another of the UN-designated safe areas, only four UN observers were in Gorazde when the attack began. Within 10 days, the Bosnian Serb assault had killed 67 people and had wounded 325, almost all of them civilians.

The attack on Gorazde moved the international community beyond threats. U.S. warplanes, acting under joint NATO and UN command, bombed Bosnian Serb positions around Gorazde. But this light display of force was not enough to keep Bosnian Serb troops from advancing on the city. In apparent retaliation for the NATO strikes, Bosnian Serb troops detained UN workers at gunpoint and forcibly confined them to their quarters. During their brief occupation of Gorazde, Bosnian Serb forces destroyed houses and buildings in and around the city.

The Gorazde incident smashed the notion that the war in Bosnia was winding down. In addition, it showed that air strikes alone were not going to defeat the Bosnian Serbs. The attack on Gorazde also made it clear that the UN could not protect the safe havens. "The so-called safe area has become the most unsafe place in the world," proclaimed an angry Izetbegovic, who was convinced that the only option for the Bosnian government was to keep fighting. The UN, which already had 33,000 troops in the former Yugoslavia, raised the authorized level to 45,000

In the aftermath of Gorazde, five nations that had been drawn deeply into Bosnia—the United States, Russia, Britain, France, and Germany—formed the Contact Group to make a fresh attempt at a peace settlement. In May 1994, the Contact Group unveiled its proposal, which handed 49 percent of Bosnian territory to the Bosnian Serbs, the other 51 percent to the Bosnian Muslim-Bosnian Croat alliance. In July 1994, the Bosnian Muslims and Bosnian Croats accepted the Contact Group's plan. Two days later, the Bosnian Serbs—who still controlled almost 70 percent of Bosnian territory—rejected it.

The plan's failure did, however, mark a small turning point in the conflict.

Control of the Media

Although guns and tanks were the main instruments of destruction in the Bosnian war, propaganda was the most important weapon in the Bosnian Serb war effort. Throughout the war, the Bosnian Serb leadership used propaganda to convince their public that they were fighting a coalition of the Ustasha and the Mujahedin (Islamic holy warriors), who were engaged in a Jihad (the Muslim term for a holy war) against all Serbs.

Before the start of the war, Bosnian Serb authorities seized television and radio transmitters in the Serbian Autonomous Regions. This left the public in these regions with only two choices for coverage of the war—Bosnian Serb media from Pale, or Serbian media from Belgrade. Bosnian Serb authorities censored the media to prevent the appearance of any unfavorable stories. Footage of ethnic cleansing was never shown on Bosnian Serb television. Foreign reporters found that Bosnian Serbs believed nearly every act of violence committed by a Serbian trooper had been an act of self-defense.

Slobodan Milosevic had pressured the Bosnian Serbs to accept the plan because he was desperate to end the UN embargo of Yugoslavia. He further resented the fact that the Bosnian Serbs were defying his wishes. After the Bosnian Serbs rejected the peace plan, Milosevic cut off Serbian support for the Bosnian Serbs. Although many believe that the Bosnian Serbs continued to receive military supplies, the blockade marked a break between Serbs in Serbia and Bosnia.

In August and September, NATO planes again bombed Serb targets, although the missions were carefully minimized and even described by NATO as "pinpricks." These minor operations failed to intimidate the Bosnian Serbs, who in November launched a major assault on Bihac. An isolated enclave of Muslim control in westernmost Bosnia, Bihac was sandwiched between the Serb-controlled area of Croatia and the Serb-controlled area of Bosnia. The Bosnian army had been making significant territorial gains

As a result, the Serbs in Bosnia and in Serbia were surprised and hurt to discover that they were portrayed in the European and U.S. media as savage aggressors. They insisted that their motives were misunderstood. In Croatia, they said, the Serbs took a stand against fascism. In Bosnia they fought against Muslim fundamentalism. When international human-rights groups denounced the Bosnian Serbs for operating detention camps and rape camps, they replied that a few isolated incidents had been blown out of proportion.

David Rieff, an American writer who acknowledged that his months in Bosnia left him siding with the Bosnian Muslims, wrote:

"If you are told over and over again that your comrades are being castrated, roasted alive on spits and drowned in their own blood . . . it is a foregone conclusion that before too long you will . . . reply in kind."

Media control was a tactic also used by the Bosnian Croats and the Bosnian Muslims throughout the war.

around Bihac, triggering a huge counterattack by the Bosnian Serbs. NATO planes flew two bombing missions—against the wishes of the UN—but failed to stop the Bosnian Serb advance. Bosnian Serb forces then took about 450 UN troops hostage.

The international efforts to help the situation were in disarray. The warring parties had rejected every initiative that the international community had put on the table. Every strategy adopted by the United States, the UN, or NATO had failed to achieve its intended results. Furthermore, NATO and the UN were at odds over how much force to use against the Bosnian Serbs. NATO leaders, recognizing that limited air strikes were not deterring Bosnian Serb aggression, supported more substantial force. The UN felt that such force would compromise its position as a neutral party and endanger its troops.

Around Christmas former U.S. president Jimmy Carter helped the warring sides negotiate a cease-fire that would take effect January 1, 1995.

But Bosnian army troops broke the cease-fire six weeks early. The warring parties entered the spring in fighting moods, and both sides expressed their contempt for the outsiders whose meetings and resolutions had had so little effect. Radovan Karadzic promised to settle all questions on the field of battle. "We will even take the cities protected by the UN," he pledged. The Bosnian government had also come to view the UN troops as a hindrance with little role to play. "The UN is keeping a peace which does not exist," said the Bosnian prime minister Haris Silajdzic.

In July 1995, the Bosnian Serbs renewed their attack on Srebrenica. This time they overran the city, taking Dutch UN soldiers hostage, executing thousands of Bosnian Muslim men, and forcibly removing women and children. Many civilians were killed as they tried to reach government-held territory. The attack on Srebrenica was one of the largest single acts of ethnic cleansing during the war. After the attack, more than 7,000 people were unaccounted for and were presumed dead. A few weeks

In August 1995, a group of Bosnian Muslims carried their belongings as they awaited transportation to government-controlled territory. Nearly 20,000 refugees fled Srebrenica when it was overrun by the Bosnian Serbs.

later, the Bosnian Serbs took the town of Zepa, another safe area. These defeats completely exposed the international community's inability to defend the safe areas.

THE TIDE TURNS

By midsummer of 1995, the situation in Bosnia stood almost where it had been early in the war. The Bosnian Serbs still held two-thirds of Bosnia. They had surrounded the safe areas and were continuing to besiege Sarajevo. The international community could not agree on the use of force against the Bosnian Serbs. The conflict had turned almost half of the prewar population of Bosnia into refugees, many of whom were huddled in various unsustainable situations inside the republic.

Then, in rapid succession, several incidents changed the picture. The turning point began with the recapture of the Croatian Krajina by Croatian forces. After three years of truce, during which the government of Croatia had bitterly tolerated the loss of the Krajina, the Croatian military unleashed a massive counter-invasion in August of 1995. As a result of the offensive, the vast majority of the area's Serbs fled into Serb-held territory in Bosnia or into Serbia itself, creating an overwhelming refugee crisis in both places. UN officials reported that Croatian soldiers were burning Serbian villages and murdering civilians.

While they tried to deal with that situation, the Bosnian Serbs also faced a fierce new offensive by the Bosnian army, whose fighting capability was vastly improved. The Bosnian army began to capture some of the territory the Bosnian Serbs had held since early in the war. The offensive forced thousands of Bosnian Serb civilians from their homes. Bosnian Serb forces responded by shelling some of the safe areas, including Sarajevo.

Meanwhile, the United States assumed a stronger role in the international effort to end the Bosnian war, and NATO finally showed a serious, sustained display of force. After Bosnian Serb forces shelled a Sarajevo marketplace, killing 43 civilians, NATO took action. This time, NATO did not settle for pinprick bombing to demonstrate its resolve. With U.S. planes making up more than half of the strike force, NATO bombed Bosnian Serb positions throughout the republic. Pinned down by the bombing, the Bosnian Serbs couldn't handle a joint offensive by the Bosnian Muslim and Bosnian Croat forces, which captured thousands of square miles of ter-

ritory. This time, Milosevic kept his oft-broken promises to the UN not to aid the Bosnian Serbs.

The Bosnian Muslim-Bosnian Croat offensive began to close in on Banja Luka, the largest city held by the Bosnian Serbs. The United States, which had barely disguised its satisfaction at the success of the offensive, worried publicly that a Bosnian Muslim capture of Banja Luka could place irresistible pressure on Milosevic to aid his Serbian compatriots. Assistant U. S. Secretary of State Richard Holbrooke, President

Clinton's negotiator in Bosnia, leaned hard and successfully on the Bosnian Muslim and Bosnian Croat leadership not to enter Banja Luka.

In a matter of weeks, though, the combined forces had increased the territory they controlled from 30 percent to 50 percent. The change meant that the 51–49 percent split that the Contact Group had been pushing for a year suddenly matched the situation on the ground. Instead of deciding whether to give up some territory to consolidate their gains, the Bosnian Serbs were faced with the prospect of losing everything if they did not agree to a new peace plan.

THE DAYTON ACCORDS

On October 5, 1995, all the parties involved in the Bosnian conflict agreed to a 60-day truce and to participation in peace talks in Dayton, Ohio, on November 1. Milosevic, who had become more interested in ending the war and the economic sanctions against Yugoslavia than in pursuing his vision of a greater Serbia, represented the Bosnian Serbs. Bosnian president Alija Izetbegovic represented the Bosnian

A Bosnian Serb soldier waves goodbye to his wife and child. As the Muslim-Croat offensive began to recapture territory from the Bosnian Serbs in the fall of 1995, thousands of Bosnian Serbs were forced to flee.

government. And Croatian president Franjo Tudjman spoke for the Bosnian Croats.

The peace talks lasted three weeks. For four days at the end, arguments raged, nerves were frayed, sleep was scarce, and failure looked certain. Just two hours before an agreement was announced, the Clinton administration drafted a statement explaining the collapse of the talks. But on November 21, the warring parties signed a deal.

The Dayton Accords retained Bosnia as a nation, with a three-member presidency and a national government. But the agreement also effectively split the republic into two roughly equal parts, with 51 percent to be primarily inhabited and governed by the Bosnian Serbs and the other 49 percent to be inhabited and governed by the Bosnian Muslim-Bosnian Croat federation. The agreement also handed Sarajevo over to the federation. In addition, the Dayton peace agreement guaranteed that those who had been ethnically cleansed had a right to return to their former homes. Some dismissed this provision as impractical. Who, they argued, would return to a village in which their ethnic group would be outnumbered?

NATO agreed to send 60,000 troops into Bosnia to help the warring parties stay apart and to launch the quest for coexistence. About 20,000 of the ground troops would be U.S. forces based at Tuzla, and they would provide dominant portions of the air and

Presidents Milosevic, Izetbegovic, and Tudjman, prepare to sign the papers for the Dayton peace plan. Seated with them is U.S. Secretary of State Warren Christopher.

naval forces. French and British troops would patrol two other zones. Dozens of countries contributed token numbers to operate under the guidance of NATO.

The Bosnian parties all pledged to cooperate with the International War Crimes Tribunal, and those under indictment for war crimes— including Radovan Karadzic and his top military leader, General Ratko Mladic—were barred from holding political office. In fact, Karadzic and Mladic didn't participate in the Dayton peace talks because they would have been arrested. Milosevic, whose critics argued that he, too, should be indicted for his role in starting the war, was instead rewarded for his role in making the peace when the UN suspended some of the sanctions against Yugoslavia.

In December 1995, Bosnian Serb demonstrators showed their contempt for the U.S.-negotiated peace plan by stomping on a U.S. flag. Many Bosnian Serbs were angry that Sarajevo had been handed over to the Muslim-Croat federation.

For all its publicly acknowledged success, the agreement satisfied none of the warring parties. The Bosnian Serbs felt Milosevic had sold them out but had no realistic way to continue the war. The Bosnian Croats had to abandon their hopes of joining Croatia. For the Bosnian Muslims and those Bosnians who had dreamed of preserving Bosnia as a multiethnic republic, it seemed the dream had been betrayed. "My government is taking part in this agreement not with any enthusiasm, but as someone taking a bitter potion of medication," said President Izetbegovic when the accord was formally signed in Paris on December 14, 1995.

The signing of the Dayton agreement enabled the international community to prevent further bloodshed. But the war had taken a great toll on Bosnia. Four years of fighting had killed an estimated 263,000 people, and had uprooted two-thirds of the country's pre-war population of 4.5 million. In addition the conflict had destroyed an estimated 25 percent of industrial facilities and infrastructure and had caused the loss of an even greater amount of housing and property. ⊕

A Critical Assessment

After the fall of Communism and the Desert Storm operation of 1991, when a U.S.-led, UN-sanctioned force rescued Kuwait from Iraqi occupation, world leaders talked a lot about a "new world order." In this new world order, UN resolutions would be respected and international law would be enforced—by the power of world opinion where possible and by multinational armed force where necessary.

Bosnia became the next great test of this idea. The UN passed more than 50 resolutions on Bosnia, but none stopped the fighting. UN peacekeeping troops served in Bosnia for three years, but ethnic cleansing still occurred. The EU convened meeting after meeting in the search for peace, and emissaries for the UN and the EU proposed several settlements. NATO repeatedly threatened to intervene with force. The United States seemed to go through a dozen Bosnian policies. But the war continued.

Ultimately the war in Bosnia became a case study of an issue that the world's great powers, the large international organizations, and especially the United States may face many times in the post-Cold War world. When should outside parties intervene in what is essentially a local war? Which outside parties should participate? And how?

Many critics have suggested that the major European powers blundered at the beginning of the Yugoslav crisis and may have missed their chance to avert the carnage that followed. Although the European powers consistently supported a united Yugoslavia during the Cold War years, that support gradually faded as tensions in the federation became apparent. As a result, Slovenia and Croatia believed that they had support for their desire to leave the federation. The critics have suggested that the European powers should have clearly told these republics that the breakup of the Yugoslav federation would be tolerated only under planned and controlled circumstances. The breakup would have to preserve existing borders, would have to follow democratic norms, would have to guarantee respect for all minority ethnic groups and, above all, would have to prevent a bloody civil war. By the time the European powers did make such a statement, the violent breakdown had already begun.

The next mistake, according to critics of the international community's performance in Bosnia, was that the UN Security Council was too slow and too tentative in extending UNPROFOR's mission into Bosnia. President Izetbegovic asked for UN peacekeepers before the fighting started, but the UN refused the request.

Meanwhile, in hopes of preventing an escalation of the crisis, the UN had imposed a worldwide embargo on arms shipments to the republics of the former Yugoslavia. But the critics denounced the embargo because it froze in place the weapons imbalance between the Bosnian Serbs and the Bosnian government. Then the UN used economic sanctions to try to pressure Serbia to stop arming, funding, and encouraging the Serbs of Bosnia and Croatia. In September, convinced that Serbia was encouraging the slaughter in Bosnia, the UN expelled Yugoslavia—the only expulsion of a member-state in UN history. None of these actions had any effect on the war.

After the war in Bosnia began, there were refugees aplenty. And the United Nations High Commissioner for Refugees (UNHCR) opened operations in Bosnia. When the Bosnian Serb militias started hijacking or blocking UN relief trucks and made it impossible for UN planes carrying relief supplies to land in Sarajevo, the Security Council sent UNPROFOR troops into Bosnia. Their limited mission was to protect the humanitarian workers and enable them to do their work.

Throughout their stay in Bosnia, UNPROFOR troops did little to stop the carnage in Bosnia. As a neutral party in the conflict, they could only shoot back if they were targets of an assault. So they could not protect or defend the victims of aggression. In addition, the Bosnian Serb forces made it clear they wouldn't let UNPROFOR get in their way.

Critics of the UN's effort complained that the UN mandate—to help the refugees but not to stop the war that was creating the refugees—was not enough. These critics felt that the UN troops should have had a more vigorous mandate to identify and punish the aggressor, to liberate territory that was taken by conquest, and to use whatever force was necessary to bring a just peace.

UN officials have answered critics by saying that peacemaking requires neutrality. They claim that the UN's job is not to take sides in a war but rather is to provide humanitarian relief, to encourage negotiated settlements, to denounce violations of international law, and to express the opinion of the world—all of which the UN did in Bosnia. Early in the conflict, the UN and the EU announced that they would not accept the violent dismemberment of Bosnia, nor would they recognize any territorial gains that occurred by conquest. They further demanded the closure of all camps at which prisoners were being mistreated and insisted on the free flow of humanitarian aid.

Finally, some observers have criticized the European powers and the United States for their reluctance to intervene militarily or to end the arms embargo. When the trouble first started, the U.S. administration of George Bush seemed to want to use Yugoslavia's crisis to reiterate that the United States is not the world's policeman. Although the Bush administration made some suggestions and supported major UN actions, it let its European allies take the lead and contributed no troops to UNPROFOR.

During the 1992 presidential campaign, candidate Bill Clinton advocated a more muscular U.S. role, but during the first 18 months of Clinton's presidency, he seemed as reluctant as Bush had been to be drawn into Bosnia. He continued, as Bush had, to rule out U.S. ground troops in Bosnia. Clinton and his diplomats urged the European powers to consider using NATO air power more aggressively, but the Europeans turned down the suggestion. Britain and France, which each had several thousand troops in Bosnia, argued that bombing would provoke a Serbian retaliation against UNPROFOR. When NATO finally agreed that more force was necessary, the UN was reluctant to approve the use of such force. Many feel that the inability to devise a plan of action encouraged the warring parties to keep fighting.

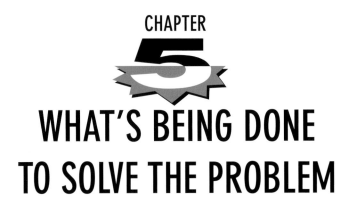

WHAT'S BEING DONE TO SOLVE THE PROBLEM

The 1995 Dayton Accords brought an end to the Bosnian war, but the agreement could not remove the hostilities that continue to simmer between Bosnia's ethnic groups. Although Bosnian Serbs, Bosnian Croats, and Bosnian Muslims had been able to live together for decades, the bloodshed of the 1990s nearly destroyed hopes for a multiethnic Bosnia. Many Bosnians do not want to return to their former homes and have chosen instead to create communities based on ethnicity. The economy is in ruins, and jobs are scarce. All sides distrust one another. In addition, Bosnia's politicians have continued to bicker over the implementation of the Dayton Accords.

THE POLITICIANS
One of the main goals of the

Like many towns throughout Bosnia, this Sarajevo neighborhood bears the scars of the conflict.

Dayton Accords was to alter the political situation through national and municipal elections. Under the agreements, all Bosnian citizens were to elect a three-person presidency, made up of one Bos-

nian Serb, one Bosnian Croat, and one Bosnian Muslim; a national parliament; and separate assemblies for the Republika Srpska and for the Federation of Bosnia and Herzegovina. The Republika

Srpska would also have its own president, whose role would be similar to that of a governor. The collective presidency would handle all foreign policy and trade issues and would be responsible for rebuilding a multiethnic Bosnia.

In September 1996, elections for the collective presidency took place. Alija Izetbegovic, as the top vote-getter, became the chairperson of the presidency. Momcilo Krajisnik, a top aide to Radovan Karadzic, won the Bosnian Serb seat, and Kresimir Zubak won the seat reserved for a Bosnian Croat. Voters in the Republika Srpska chose Biljana Plavsic as the president of the Bosnian Serbs. The elections were held without violence, but the results were a victory for the nationalist parties who wanted to maintain the ethnic partition of the country. Opposition parties striving for a multiethnic state received little access to media coverage. Supporters of the nationalist parties intimidated and physically abused many opposition candidates prior to the elections.

The members of the three-person presidency have not shown much enthusiasm for working together. Since the elections, they have repeatedly argued over even the smallest details, including where to hold their meetings. Krajisnik boycotted the presidency after its first meeting, complaining about lack of security in Sarajevo. And, because all three members are unhappy with the Dayton Accords, they have been slow to implement its measures. The politicians' inability to cooperate has set the tone for attempts at reconciliation throughout Bosnia. The ethnic boundaries have only hardened.

Meanwhile, Karadzic, who was barred from the political process and had agreed to withdraw from public life as part of the Dayton Accords, continues to hold power among Bosnian Serbs. This situation has created a new conflict among the Bosnian Serb leadership. During the war, Biljana Plavsic had been a loyal Karadzic supporter and an advocate of ethnic cleansing. Since she has become the president of the

© Kodia Photo & Graphics

The power struggle between Radovan Karadzic (left) *and Biljana Plavsic* (second from left) *has created tensions within the Republika Srpska leadership. Plavsic, who was elected as president of the Republika Srpska in 1996, has accused Karadzic of corruption and profiting from the war.*

The peace agreement signed in Dayton awarded the Federation of Bosnia and Herzegovina 51 percent of Bosnian territory, including the capital of Sarajevo and corridor leading to the Muslim enclave of Gorazde. The Bosnian Serbs received the other 49 percent of the land, an amount much smaller than they had hoped for. Nearly 60,000 troops from 32 countries were sent to maintain peace between the two entities and oversee the implementation of the peace agreement.

Republika Srpska, however, Plavsic has turned against Karadzic, accusing him of corruption. While many Bosnian Serb nationalists still support Karadzic, Plavsic and her supporters are backing the Dayton Accords, which they hope will bring much needed reconstruction aid.

Municipal elections have also created a stumbling block for the peace agreement. The Organization for Security and Cooperation in Europe (OSCE), which was charged with supervising the elections, had to postpone them twice for fear that the outcome would be unfairly weighted towards the nationalist parties. One problem was that many refugees had not been allowed to return to their prewar homes. In addition, OSCE officials believed that all parties were trying to manipulate the elections by registering people to vote in municipalities where they did not live. To combat these problems, OSCE began a positive registration campaign so that voters would have to prove that they were eligible to vote in a particular municipality.

Despite the threats of hard-line nationalists on all sides, local elections were held in September 1997. NATO troops created and patrolled a route that allowed displaced citizens to return to vote in their former homes. The strange result is that cities that no longer have a Bosnian Muslim population elected a number of Bosnian Muslim representatives to serve on city councils. Similarly, voters chose Bosnian Serbs to represent areas that no longer have a Bosnian Serb population. The hope is that mixed city and municipal councils will help to reverse the effects of ethnic cleansing. But many feel that these elections will do little to change the situation in Bosnia.

The Growth of Muslim Nationalism

When the war began, the Muslim-led Bosnian government sought to maintain a sovereign, multiethnic Bosnia. But as the conflict progressed, an increasing sense of isolation began to take hold among Bosnia's Muslims. The international community's recognition of the territorial claims of the Bosnian Serbs and support of the UN weapons embargo bewildered President Izetbegovic and other Muslim leaders, and left many Bosnian Muslims feeling betrayed. As a result, the war and the subsequent peace agreement created among Bosnian Muslims a stronger sense of nationalism than had existed before.

Since the end of the war, Muslim nationalism has continued to grow. Interest in fundamentalist Islamic tradition, which is much stricter than the Bosnian form of Islam, has risen. Whereas Bosnian Muslims once celebrated the republic's mixed character, now many endorse the separation of Bosnia's ethnic groups and the creation of ethnic enclaves. The Muslim leadership has also turned to Iran for military support, a move that many observers feel could lead to the creation of a more militant Islamic community in Bosnia.

Two men, one in Islamic dress, walk by the Iranian cultural center in Sarajevo.

In early 1996, Bosnian Serb residents prepared to leave the Sarajevo suburb of Ilidza—which had been held by Bosnian Serb forces throughout the war—before it was handed over to the Muslim-Croat federation.

© Russell Gordon/Zuma Press Inc.

A TORN SOCIETY

Although the Dayton Accords maintained Bosnia as a single entity, the country is essentially divided. The Federation of Bosnia and Herzegovina and the Republika Srpska coexist in an uneasy truce. Movement across the boundary lines is limited, and there is almost no communication by mail or phone. Both entities have separate flags and currencies. The hardened boundary reflects the feelings of many Bosnians. All sides feel as if they were the victims of the war.

A perfect example of the bitter feelings created by the war and the peace agreement appeared in once-harmonious Sarajevo, which is under the control of the Federation of Bosnia and Herzegovina. When the city and its suburbs reverted to federation control, many Bosnian Serb residents left in a mass exodus. Some even dug up the bodies of their dead ancestors to take them to Bosnian Serb territory. In the suburb of Ilidza, a number of Bosnian Serb doctors and health workers stayed behind, pledging to work with the new government and help rebuild Bosnia. Within a few weeks, however, the government fired the doctors. International mediators believed that Bosnian Muslim nationalists spearheaded the action.

In towns and villages throughout Bosnia, numerous conflicts have arisen when refugees have tried to return to their former homes. In the village of Mahala, part of Republika Srpska, Bosnian Serbs attacked Bosnian Muslims who were attempting to rebuild their bombed out and abandoned village. In the

> *"I used to live in the Muslim part of Bosnia, but I never considered going back there to vote . . . This is where our state is . . . The Muslims will stay on their side and we will stay on ours."*

town of Vogosca, Muslims stoned Bosnian Serbs who were visiting their old homes. And, despite the truce that was signed in 1994, tension between Bosnian Muslims and Bosnian Croats remains. In the divided city of Mostar, hardline Muslims and Croats have resisted all efforts to reunify the two ethnic groups.

Whose History Is It?

To see an example of how the war has altered Bosnian society, take a look at the recent history textbooks for Bosnian students. In the same way that towns and villages around Bosnia are becoming segregated by ethnic group, so are schools. Even within mixed schools, students are being placed in separate classrooms. And each group has its own version of history.

The Serbian Ministry of Education in Belgrade publishes the history texts for Bosnian Serb students. These books claim that there never really was a Bosnia. Instead, they refer to the republic as Serbian territory that the Ottoman Empire took over. The books portray the centuries spent under Ottoman rule as an age of brutal occupation. Gavrilo Princip, the assassin of Archduke Franz Ferdinand, becomes a Serbian hero. And the most recent Bosnian war becomes a campaign of genocide by Muslims.

Bosnian Croat students learn a different history. Their textbooks, which are published in the Croatian capital of Zagreb, state that Bosnia is really part of Croatia and that the Kingdom of the Serbs, Croats, and Slovenes was actually a plot to create a greater Serbia. These history books briefly mention the Ustasha genocide during World War II, but focus more on atrocities committed by the Chetniks. In the recent conflict, according to these books, Croatian forces fought against Serbian and Muslim aggression.

Finally, Bosnian Muslim students are taught an even different history. Their textbooks describe the Ottoman era as an age of enlightenment. The period between the two world wars becomes a time of oppression for Bosnia's Muslims. Crimes committed by Bosnian Muslims during World War II go unmentioned. These books depict the Bosnian war as an attack against Bosnia by the Serbs.

THE SEARCH FOR WAR CRIMINALS

The International War Crimes Tribunal, established in 1993, investigates and prosecutes war crimes in the former Yugoslavia. The tribunal has identified war crimes as genocide—the systematic killing or harming of members of a national, ethnic, racial, or religious group with the obvious intent of destroying it—and crimes against humanity, which include rape and torture. Since the Dayton Accords, the tribunal has been trying to track down Bosnian war criminals, an effort that many hope will help to heal Bosnia's wounds. By pursuing the individuals responsible for wartime atrocities, the tribunal hopes that victims will feel less need to take revenge into their own hands.

But bringing the war criminals to justice has been quite difficult. By late 1997, the tribunal had charged 78 individuals with war crimes—57 Bosnian Serbs, 18 Bosnian Croats, and 3 Bosnian Muslims. Of the 78 individuals so charged, only a handful have been caught. Others remain free and sometimes in positions of authority.

CONGRES MONDIAL SERBE
WORLD SERB CONGRESS
WELTKONGRESS DER SERBEN

др Радован Караџић

НАСТАВЉАМО !

© Leif Skoogfors/Zuma Press Inc.

A poster in the Republika Srpska pledges support for Radovan Karadzic, whose forced retirement from politics did not diminish his political power. Many observers believe that an attempt to arrest him for war crimes could lead to widespread violence in the Republika Srpska.

Although NATO-led forces have recently made attempts to capture war criminals, many Bosnians have complained that they have not done enough.

The case of Radovan Karadzic, whom the tribunal has charged with two counts of genocide, highlights the problem. Generally recognized as one of the architects of ethnic cleansing, Karadzic remains a powerful figure for Bosnian Serbs. He still has a great deal of political control. The peacekeeping troops say that they would arrest him if they could find him, yet Karadzic reports every day to an office in the town of Pale. NATO leaders have asked Serbian president Milosevic to hand Karadzic over to the tribunal, but so far Milosevic has refused.

The tribunal has had some success, however. In its first trial, prosecutors convicted Dusko Tadic, a Bosnian Serb accused of rounding up Bosnian Muslims and Bosnian Croats for ethnic cleansing. Even though the tribunal viewed Tadic as a small player in the conflict, the prosecution's goal is to convict those who carried out crimes so it can get to the people who ordered the crimes. In October 1997, 10 Bosnian Croats charged with war crimes surrendered to the tribunal. In addition, all three indicted (charged) Bosnian Muslims are on trial.

In the meantime, UN investigators have been inspecting mass gravesites for evidence to be used in prosecuting war criminals. At a site near Srebrenica, investigators found 154 skeletons in civilian clothing. The investigators believed them to be the victims of the Bosnian Serb attack on Srebrenica in 1995.

THE PEACEKEEPERS

Since December 20, 1995, when the UN officially transferred control of the peacekeeping duties to NATO, NATO-led forces have had a major role in enforcing the Dayton Accords. So far, the NATO-led troops have successfully stationed themselves between the warring parties. But there have been setbacks along the way. Each of the Bosnian ethnic groups has complained that the others have been violating the requirements for letting refugees return home or for releasing prisoners of war. In January of 1996, a couple of Bosnian Serb officers ac-

cidentally drove into Bosnian Muslim territory. Bosnian Muslims accused the two of war crimes, even though they were not wanted by the international tribunal. The Bosnian Serb forces cut off their contact with NATO to protest the continued holding of those officers.

Recently, the NATO-led forces have taken on a more active role in enforcing the Dayton Accords by pursuing war criminals and preventing the spread of propaganda. For example, in July 1997, British troops went after two Bosnian Serb war criminals, arresting one and killing the other in a shootout. In August soldiers

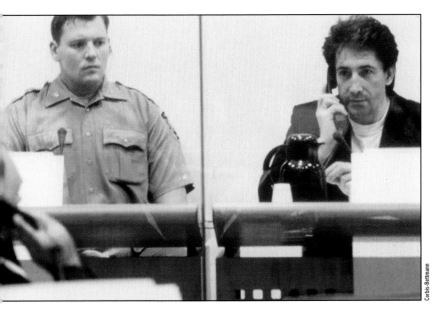

Corbis-Bettmann

Bosnian Serb war criminal Dusko Tadic talks to his lawyer during his trial. Tadic was convicted and sentenced to 20 years in prison. Although the war crimes tribunal has had some success, many Bosnian war criminals are still at large.

seized a police station where pro-Karadzic police forces had been storing weapons. NATO-led forces later took control of TV transmitters belonging to Bosnian Serbs who supported Karadzic. The transmitters were being used to broadcast inflammatory messages against the Dayton Accords and against supporters of Bosnian Serb president Plavsic.

HUMANITARIAN EFFORTS

Rebuilding a peaceful, multi-ethnic Bosnia will be a long and difficult task. With the politicians still quarreling, there is a strong chance that renewed hostilities could erupt. Yet amid all the evidence of ethnic nationalism, there is a new sense of hope among some Bosnians that peace can be achieved through reconciliation and

© NATO Photos

At this checkpoint in Sarajevo, Italian peacekeeping troops monitor movement in and out of the city.

BOSNIA *Fractured Region*

cooperation. Although they face tremendous odds, a variety of local and international organizations are working to create peaceful communities in which Bosnian Serbs, Bosnian Croats, and Bosnian Muslims can live together.

One such organization is the American Refugee Committee (ARC), headquartered in Minneapolis, Minnesota. Operating mainly in seven sites throughout Bosnia, ARC promotes repatriation, reconciliation, and self-sufficiency through projects that include reconstruction of houses, schools, and clinics; community development; and health care. In Sarajevo, ARC is rebuilding preschools and playgrounds that were destroyed during the fighting. The organization's main goal is to encourage refugees from the war to return to their old homes, even in areas that were ethnically cleansed.

ARC's efforts at reconciliation and repatriation have run into roadblocks. Many refugees are afraid to return to their old homes for fear of future persecution. In other cases, local town governments dominated by a

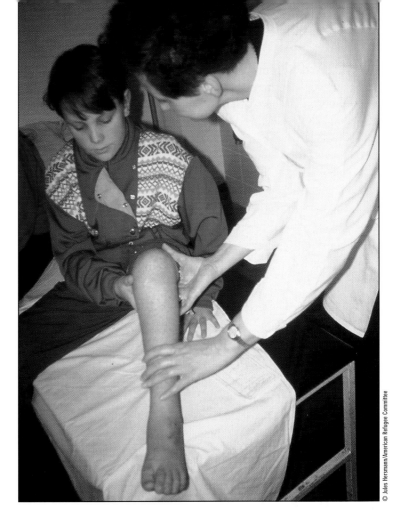

A doctor attends to a young Bosnian refugee. In addition to reconciliation and repatriation efforts, the American Refugee Committee also provides health care for Bosnian refugees.

single ethnic group have prevented the return of refugees from other ethnic groups.

Another group in Bosnia that is promoting peace through reconciliation is Conflict Resolution Catalysts (CRC). An international organization based in Montpelier, Vermont, CRC has established two programs in Bosnia. The People Connection Project links international volunteers with local citizen's groups on all sides of the conflict. The volunteers teach the participants how to resolve conflicts and disputes through nonviolent methods and assist in developing a culture of peace and democracy. To facilitate the project, CRC has opened community centers in Sarajevo and Banja Luka that provide a place for people of all ethnic groups to rebuild relationships and to learn conflict-resolution skills. CRC volunteers have also worked with local educators to develop conflict resolution and peace curricula in Bosnian schools. The Neighborhood Facilitators Project creates opportunities for Bosnian citizens to resolve conflicts at the neighborhood level. These efforts enable Bosnian citizens to become local peacemakers, who are then able to network with local authorities to address citizen concerns.

CRC also places a special emphasis on working with Bosnian children, many of whom have grown up knowing only conflict. *Balkan Youth Bridge* is a monthly journal that Bosnian youth of all ethnic groups write, edit, and produce. At the Banja Luka community center, volunteers are teaching Bosnian children how to be disc jockey's for the local radio station. CRC has also created youth programs that offer counseling and support.

Programs such as these are allowing Bosnian citizens to take an active role in the rebuilding of their country. Although CRC has used international volunteers to get these programs off the ground, it is also training Bosnians to take them over. A measure of its success is that the People Connection

Project has developed into a locally run organization independent from CRC.

In some Bosnian communities friendships are overcoming the forces of ethnic nationalism. In the town of Orasje, along the border with Croatia, Bosnian Muslims, Bosnian Serbs, and Bosnian Croats are learning again how to live together peacefully. Even though the town is nearly 90 percent Croatian, Bosnian Serbs and Muslims are treated fairly. "We've learned to be more moderate," says a local Bosnian Muslim leader.

The future of Bosnia-Herzegovina is uncertain. Although the architects of the Dayton Accords hope that they have created a lasting agreement, a true peace has not yet been found. The real issue is whether or not the country and its people can move beyond the destruction of the recent conflict. Can Bosnia break free of its history? Or will the forces of ethnic nationalism once again cause neighbors to fight against one another?

For peace to succeed in Bosnia, the Bosnians who want peace must find a way to confront the issues that led to ethnic conflict. They must embrace solutions that don't involve weapons or

> *"In this chorus for peace today we also hear the hallowed voices of the victims—the children whose playgrounds were shelled in the killing, the young girls brutalized by rape, the men shot down in mass graves. . . those who died in battle."*
> *—U.S. President Bill Clinton*

ethnic cleansing. And they must recognize that continuing this conflict may completely destroy the country for future generations. ⊕

Despite continuing tensions, many Bosnians are trying to put the conflict behind them and to move on with their lives. In Mostar (above), *residents are trying to rebuild an Ottoman-era bridge that once symbolized the unity of Bosnia's different ethnic groups. In the town of Novi Travnik* (left), *a Bosnian Serb, a Bosnian Croat, and a Bosnian Muslim work together to repair a house.*

EPILOGUE*

By mid-1998, the major issues dividing Bosnia had not changed. The two entities that make up the country remain separate. Only 34,000 refugees have returned to territory that is occupied by an opposing group. Local authorities have failed to live up to promises of fair treatment toward all ethnic groups. No major violence has erupted since the end of the war, but U.S. and NATO troops plan to stay in Bosnia throughout 1998. U.S. and European leaders feel that a military presence might be needed in Bosnia for years to come.

But there is hope in Bosnia. Led by Carlos Westendorp, the main representative of the international peacekeeping efforts, the peacekeepers are slowly gaining power over the local politicians who want to obstruct the Dayton Accords. Westendorp has pressured politicians from both entities who are trying to prevent refugees from returning to their homes. He has also designed new currency for the country and a new Bosnian flag. In addition, NATO-led troops have made more arrests in the continuing search for war criminals. Pressure has been mounting on Radovan Karadzic to turn himself in to the International War Crimes Tribunal. Meanwhile, life is returning to normal in the war-ravaged country. In February 1998, for example, rail service started up after six years of inactivity.

In Yugoslavia, however, ethnic tensions in the province of Kosovo threaten to break out into another war. The Serbian government has sent in paramilitary police to crack down on the activities of the Kosovo Liberation Army (KLA), a paramilitary organization formed by ethnic Albanians fighting for an independent Kosovo. In March 1998, Serbian troops killed more than 80 ethnic Albanians in attacks against the KLA. This crackdown has prompted fears of new rounds of ethnic cleansing.

*Please note: The information presented in *Bosnia: Fractured Region* was current at the time of the book's publication. For the most up-to-date information on the conflict, check for articles in the international section of U.S. daily newspapers. *The Economist*, a weekly magazine, is also a good source for up-to-date information. You may also wish to access, via the internet, other sources of information about Bosnia: This Week in Bosnia Home Page, at http://www.world.std.com/~slm, the International War Crimes Tribunal Home Page, at http://www.igc.apc.org/tribunal, and the Official Election Website of the OSCE at http://www.oscebih.org.

CHRONOLOGY

A.D. **392**   Christianity becomes the official religion of the Roman Empire.

395   The Roman Empire splits into a western half and an eastern half. The eastern branch becomes known as the Byzantine Empire.

500s–600s   Slavic peoples enter the Balkans, settling in different regions. Croats settle on the western side of the empire, while Serbs settle on the eastern side.

1054   The Roman Catholic Church and the Eastern Orthodox Church split. Croats become Roman Catholics, while Serbs follow Eastern Orthodoxy.

1326   King Stefan Tvrtko annexes Herzegovina, making Bosnia-Herzegovina a single political unit.

1389   The Ottoman Turks, who follow the Islamic faith, invade Serbia. The Ottomans defeat the Serbs in the Battle of Kosovo. Despite the conquest, most Serbs refuse to convert to Islam.

1463   The Ottomans conquer Bosnia. A majority of the Bosnian nobility converts to Islam.

1541   Croatian and Hungarian nobles, trying to halt the Ottoman advance, elect Ferdinand I as king of both countries. A distinct dividing line between the Hapsburg Empire and the Ottoman Empire is created, and the Military Frontier is established.

1830   The Ottoman Empire recognizes Serbia as a principality under Turkish control.

1868   Austria-Hungary grants Croatia limited autonomy.

1877   Forces from Serbia, Russia, Romania, and Bulgaria liberate Bosnia.

1878   The Treaty of Berlin grants Serbia full independence, but awards Bosnia to Austria-Hungary, creating deep resentment among Serbs.

1908   Austria-Hungary officially annexes Bosnia as a permanent possession, further enraging the Serbs.

1912–1913 Serbia, Greece, and Bulgaria drive the Ottoman Turks out of the Balkans in the First Balkan War. Arguments over the division of Macedonia lead to the Second Balkan War.

1914   A Bosnian Serb revolutionary named Gavrilo Princip assassinates Archduke Franz Ferdinand, heir to the Hapsburg throne. Austria-Hungary, sensing that the Serbs were behind the attack, declares war on Serbia. World War I begins.

1918   World War I ends. The redrawing of the European map after the war establishes the Kingdom of the Serbs, Croats, and Slovenes. A Serbian royal family is selected to rule the country. Political and ethnic problems plague the new kingdom.

1929   The kingdom's political instability leads King Aleksander to abolish the constitution and establish a dictatorship. His attempts to reconcile Croats and Serbs and to impose political unity fail.

1934   A revolutionary supported by Croatian nationalists assassinates King Aleksander.

1939   World War II begins, pitting Nazi Germany and the Axis powers—Italy and Japan—against the Allied forces, which included Britain, France, the United States, and the Soviet Union.

1941   Bowing to pressure from Germany and the Axis powers, Yugoslavia signs the Tripartite Pact. One month later, Germany invades the country. Bosnia becomes part of an enlarged Croatian state, under the rule of fascist leader Ante Pavelic. The Ustasha regime begins a campaign to eliminate Jews, Gypsies, and Serbs. Opponents of the regime form two resistance movements—the Partisans, headed by Tito, and the Chetniks.

1945   World War II ends. The victory of the Partisans over the Axis powers and the Chetniks enables Tito to become the new leader of Yugoslavia. He establishes a Soviet-style Communist government.

1946 A new constitution establishes a federation of six republics.

1948 Tito refuses to follow the orders of Soviet leader Joseph Stalin and pulls Yugoslavia out of the Soviet bloc.

1971 The Yugoslav government officially recognizes Bosnian Muslims as an ethnic group, thereby giving them equal status with Yugoslavia's other ethnic groups

1974 Tito establishes a new constitution that divides power among the republics and provinces.

1980 Tito dies.

1987 Slobodan Milosevic becomes the president of the Serbian republic.

1990 Slovenia and Croatia become the first Yugoslav republics to legalize opposition parties and to hold multiparty elections. Later in 1990, Macedonia and Bosnia-Herzegovina hold their own multiparty elections. Citizens of Bosnia vote along ethnic lines. Alija Izetbegovic becomes the president of the republic.

1991 Croatia and Slovenia declare independence from the Yugoslav federation. After a brief conflict, Slovenia is allowed to secede. In Croatia war breaks out between Croats and ethnic Serbs living in the Croatian Krajina. In November a cease-fire is arranged, and the UN establishes UNPROFOR to keep the peace. Izetbegovic asks the UN to deploy troops in Bosnia, but his request is denied.

1992 In a public referendum held in March, Bosnia's non-Serb citizens vote for independence. Bosnia's Serbs declare their own independent state, called the Republika Srpska. By early summer, Bosnian Serb forces control two-thirds of the republic. In August British and U.S. journalists publish reports of ethnic cleansing and detention camps. In October Bosnian Muslims and Bosnian Croats break their alliance and begin fighting one another. Serbia and Montenegro form a new Yugoslavia.

1993 International negotiators present the Vance-Owen peace plan, which proposes that Bosnia to be divided into ethnic provinces. The warring parties reject the Vance-Owen plan and continue fighting. As Bosnian Serbs continue their assault, the UN Security Council declares six Bosnian cities to be safe areas. Bosnian Serb forces ignore the declaration and continue to attack these cities.

1994 A Bosnian Serb mortar attack on a Sarajevo marketplace provokes ultimatums from the UN and NATO. Bosnian Muslims agree to a truce with Bosnian Croats and the Croatian government. Negotiators introduce the Contact Group peace initiative, which all sides reject. Former U.S. president Jimmy Carter negotiates a cease-fire.

1995 The warring parties break the negotiated cease-fire six weeks early. Bosnian Serb forces overrun the city of Srebrenica, killing thousands of Bosnian Muslims. In August Croatian forces recapture the Croatian Krajina, while the combined forces of the Bosnian Croats and the Bosnian army begin to roll back Bosnian Serb gains. By October all parties agree to a truce. In November the warring parties sign the Dayton Peace agreement. The United States and NATO agree to supply troops for a peacekeeping force.

1996 Elections for the collective presidency of Bosnia-Herzegovina are held. Voters elect a three-member presidency to be headed by Alija Izetbegovic. Biljana Plavsic becomes the president of the Republika Srpska.

1997 Bosnian citizens vote for representatives in local and municipal elections, which take place with little violence. NATO peacekeeping troops take a more active role in enforcing the Dayton Accords. U.S. president Bill Clinton extends the mission of U.S. troops through 1998.

1997 Bosnia enters its third year of peace, with international representatives continuing to implement the terms of the Dayton Accords. Ethnic violence breaks out in Kosovo when Serbian police attempt to crack down on ethnic Albanians.

1998 Bosnia enters its third year of peace, with international representatives continuing to implement the terms of the Dayton Accords. Ethnic violence breaks out in Kosovo when Serbian police attempt to crack down on ethnic Albanians.

SELECTED BIBLIOGRAPHY

Curtis, Glenn E., ed. *Yugoslavia: A Country Study*. Washington, D.C.: Federal Research Division, Library of Congress, 1992.

Denitch, Bogdan. *Ethnic Nationalism: The Tragic Death of Yugoslavia*. Minneapolis: University of Minnesota Press, 1994.

Donia, Robert J., and John V.A. Fine, Jr. *Bosnia and Hercegovina: A Tradition Betrayed*. New York: Columbia University Press, 1994.

Gutman, Roy. *Witness to Genocide*. New York: Macmillan Publishing Company, 1993.

Judah, Tim. *The Serbs: History, Myth and the Destruction of Yugoslavia*. New Haven: Yale University Press, 1997.

Malcolm, Noel. *Bosnia: A Short History*. New York: New York University Press, 1994.

Rieff, David. *Slaughterhouse: Bosnia and the Failure of the West*. New York: Simon & Schuster, 1995.

Sells, Michael. *The Bridge Betrayed*. Berkeley: University of California Press, 1996.

Silber, Laura, and Allan Little. *Yugoslavia: Death of a Nation*. New York: TV Books, Inc., 1993.

Silverman, Robin Landew. *A Bosnian Family*. Minneapolis: Lerner Publications Company, 1997.

Vulliamy, Ed. *Seasons in Hell*. New York: St. Martin's Press, 1994.

Zimmerman, Warren. *Origins of a Catastrophe*. New York: Random House, 1996.

INDEX

North Atlantic Treaty Organization (NATO), 19, 66, 84; air strikes by, 69, 70–71, 72–73; troops, 74, 81.
Omarska camp, 23
Organization for Security and Cooperation in Europe (OSCE), 80–1
Ottoman Empire, 14, 32–35, 36, 39–40
Owen, David, 64
Pan-Slavism, 35–36
Partisans, 42–43, 44
People Connection Project, 88
Plavsic, Biljana, 79–80, 86
Poland, 16–17, 50
Prince Lazar, 32, 33
propaganda, 22, 70–71
rapes, 20, 23, 61
Red Cross, 23
refugees, 55, 69, 72, 82–83, 87; safe areas for, 65–66; as a result of ethnic cleansing, 22, 25, 60.
religion, 14–15, 31, 34; see also Christianity, Islam
Republic of the Serbian Krajina, 55
Republika Srpska, 18, 29, 57–59, 78–79, 82, 83
Roman Catholicism, 14, 31, 32
Roman Empire, 30, 30–1
Russia, 36, 39, 68–69
Sarajevo, 10, 15, 62, 65–66; siege of, 24–25, 59–60, 68–69
Second Balkan War in 1913, 38
Serbia, 10, 12, 31–32, 36, 38, 49; see also Bosnian Serbs
Serbian Black Hand, 38
Serbian League of Communists, 50
Serbs, 13, 14, 17, 31, 33, 35, 36, 41, 46
Slavs, 12, 14, 30–31, 32, 35–36
Slovenia, 10, 12–13, 14, 17, 54–55
South Slavs, 30–31, 35
Srebrenica, 65–66, 71
Stalin, Joseph, 44
Tadic, Dusko, 85
Tito, Marshal, 16, 42–47, 48
Treaty of Berlin, 36
Treaty of London, 38
Tripartite Pact, 41
Tudjman, Franjo, 19, 29, 52–3, 62, 74
Turkey, 12, 36, 39, 49
Turks. See Ottoman Empire
Tuzla, 10, 66, 74
United Nations (UN), 19, 25, 55, 60, 73; failure to protect safe zones, 69–70; peacekeeping efforts by, 64–69; troops, 65, 71.
United Nations High Commissioner for Refugees, 61
United Nations Protection Force (UNPROFOR), 56–61
United States, 55, 70; aid Communist Yugoslavia, 45; uses force against Bosnian Serbs, 69.

Ustasha, 40–44, 53
Vance, Cyrus, 56, 64
violence, 20–3, 27, 61, 69, 72–73; see also Bosnian conflict
war criminals, 83–85
World War I (1914–1918), 12, 39–40
World War II (1939–1945), 10, 16, 27–8, 41–4
Yugoslavia, 10, 12–13, 16–17; deterioration of, 48, 50; ethnic groups in, 13–16; formation of, 40–41; secessions from, 17, 20, 26–27, 54–55; under Tito leadership, 44–47.
Yugoslav wars, 55
Zepa, 66, 72

ABOUT THE AUTHOR

Eric Black, a journalist for the *Star Tribune* of Minneapolis-St. Paul, specializes in writing about the historical background of international situations. Black is the author of *Our Constitution: The Myth That Binds Us; Rethinking the Cold War;* and *Parallel Realities: A Jewish/Arab History of Israel/Palestine.* In 1979–1980, he was awarded an American Political Science Association Congressional Fellowship for a year of work and study in Washington, D.C. As recipient of the Knight Fellowship, he spent a year at Stanford University in 1985–1986. Black lives with his wife, Lauren Baker, and their two children, Rosie and Danny.

ABOUT THE CONSULTANTS

Andrew Bell-Fialkoff, *World in Conflict* series consultant, is a specialist on nationalism, ethnicity, and ethnic conflict. He is the author of *Ethnic Cleansing,* published by St. Martin's Press in 1996, and has written numerous articles for *Foreign Affairs* and other journals. He is currently writing a book on the role of migration in the history of the Eurasian Steppe. Bell-Fialkoff lives in Bradford, Massachusetts.

Sarah A. Kent is a specialist in East European history. She is the author of "Writing the Yugoslav Wars: English-Language Books on Bosnia (1992–1996) and the Challenges of Analyzing Contemporary History" published in the October 1997 issue of the *American Historical Review.* She is currently writing a book on the formation of the Croatian national identity in the late nineteenth century. Kent is an associate professor of history at the University of Wisconsin–Stevens Point.

SOURCES OF QUOTED MATERIAL

p. 23 Ed Vulliamy, *Seasons in Hell: Understanding Bosnia's War* (New York: St. Martin's Press, 1994), 108; p. 25 David Rieff, *Slaughterhouse: Bosnia and the Failure of the West* (New York: Simon & Schuster, 1995), 133; p. 26 Robert J. Donia and John V.A. Fine, Jr., *Bosnia & Hercegovina: A Tradition Betrayed* (New York: Columbia University Press, 1994), 264; p. 29 "Accordion Trills of Old Bosnia," *New York Times*, 9 September, 1996, A4; p. 32 Glenn E. Curtis, ed., *Yugoslavia: A Country Study* (Washington, D.C.: Federal Research Division, Library of Congress, 1992), 18; p. 37 Barbara Tuchman, *The Guns of August* (New York: Bonanza Books, 1982), 71; p. 41 Robert J. Donia and John V.A. Fine, Jr., *Bosnia & Hercegovina: A Tradition Betrayed* (New York: Columbia University Press, 1994), 121; p. 50 Glenn E. Curtis, ed., *Yugoslavia: A Country Study* (Washington, D.C.: Federal Research Division, Library of Congress, 1992), xxvi; p. 53 Misha Glenny, *The Fall of Yugoslavia* (New York: Penguin Books, 1992), 12; p. 57 "Rumor & Reality," *Time Magazine*, 24 August, 1992, 48; p. 61 News Services, "Bosnian Serbs Debate Accord," *Minneapolis Star Tribune*, 20 January, 1993, 4A; p. 66 Robert J. Donia and John V.A. Fine, Jr., *Bosnia & Hercegovina: A Tradition Betrayed* (New York: Columbia University Press, 1994), 266; p. 69 Laura Silber and Allan Little, *Yugoslavia: Death of a Nation* (New York: TV Books, Inc., 1993), 318; p. 71 David Rieff, *Slaughterhouse: Bosnia and the Failure of the West* (New York: Simon & Schuster, 1995), 113; p. 71 News Services, "Rebel Serbs Fight Back, Launch New Offensive," *Minneapolis Star Tribune*, 31 March, 1995, 7A; p. 71 Ibid; p. 75 "Balkan Foes Sign Peace Pact, Dividing an Unpacified Bosnia," *New York Times*, 15 December, 1995, A1; p. 82 "Bosnia Holds Vote with Few Reports of Real Violence," *New York Times*, 15 September, 1996; p. 88 "Accordion Trills of Old Bosnia," *New York Times*, 4 September, 1996, A4; p. 88 "Is Peace at Hand? Balkan Leaders Sign Treaty," *Minneapolis Star Tribune*, 15 December, 1995, 1A.